# Blood, Sweat and Tears

First published in 2012 by
Liberties Press
7 Rathfarnham Road | Terenure | Dublin 6W
Tel: +353 (1) 405 5701
www.libertiespress.com | info@libertiespress.com

Trade enquiries to Gill & Macmillan Distribution
Hume Avenue | Park West | Dublin 12
T: +353 (1) 500 9534 | F: +353 (1) 500 9595 | E: sales@gillmacmillan.ie

Distributed in the UK by
Turnaround Publisher Services
Unit 3 | Olympia Trading Estate | Coburg Road | London N22 6TZ
T: +44 (0) 20 8829 3000 | E: orders@turnaround-uk.com

ISBN: 978-1-907593-55-0
2 4 6 8 10 9 7 5 3 1
A CIP record for this title is available from the British Library.

Cover design by Sin É Design
Internal design by Liberties Press
Printed by ScandBook AB

# Blood, Sweat and Tears

*An Irish Soldier's Story of Love and Loss*

## Tom Clonan

# Contents

*For Aideen,*
*Darach, Eoghan, Ailbhe, Rossa*
*&*

*Our precious angel, Liadain*


*&*


*For the men and women of the 78th Battalion,*
*with whom I am proud to have served in Lebanon*

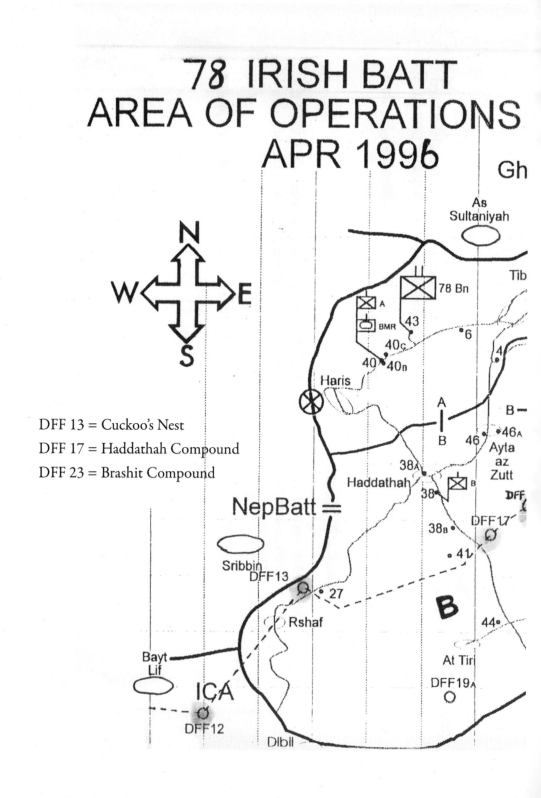

# 78 IRISH BATT
# AREA OF OPERATIONS
# APR 1996

Gh

As Sultaniyah

Tib

78 Bn

A

BMR

43

6

40c

40 40B

4

Haris

N
W E
S

A
B

B —
46A
46 Ayta
az
Zutt

DFF 13 = Cuckoo's Nest

DFF 17 = Haddathah Compound

DFF 23 = Brashit Compound

38A

Haddathah

B

38

DFF

DFF17

NepBatt =

38B

41

Sribbin
DFF13

27

B

44

Rshaf

Bayt
Lif

ICA

At Tiri

DFF19A

DFF12

Dibil

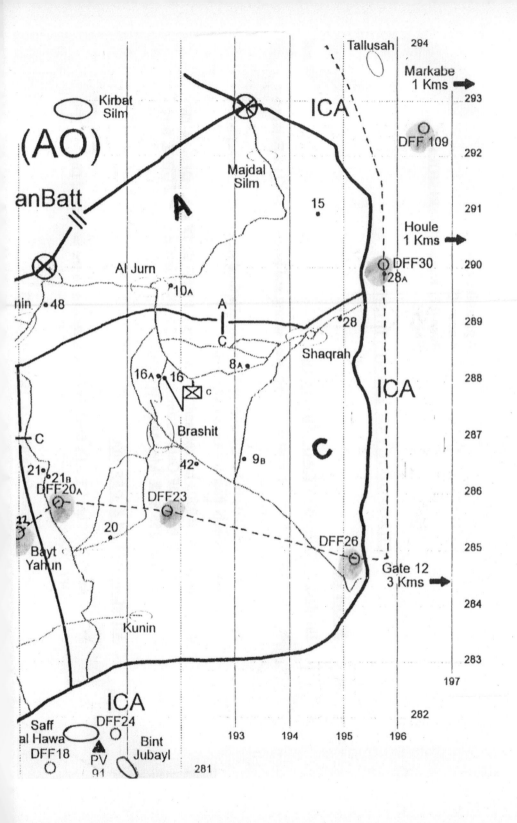

Foreword

# The Lebanon–Israeli Conflict

I kicked and squealed my way into this life in the Rotunda Hospital on Dublin's Parnell Square in the summer of 1966. As I did so, Palestinian militants crossed the border from Lebanon and infiltrated the Israeli settlement of Margaliot – known in Arabic as Hunin. In the pre-dawn darkness, they planted a series of explosive devices among the dwellings and homes of the sleeping village. Their mission – to kill as many Jewish settlers as possible. This latest action was just another in a series of hostile acts that would mark the beginning of a long and bitter cycle of violence between Lebanon and Israel. The rest, as they say, is history.

As my Mum held me that summer morning, I doubt if she was aware of unfolding events along the Lebanese-Israeli border. My Dad, a Dublin policeman based in Pearse Street Garda Station, did not have far to walk to greet me. As he made his way into the Rotunda, I doubt if he gave the Middle East a thought.

During that summer in Dublin however, a new chapter in the long and tragic history of the Middle East was opening in Lebanon. Little did my parents know then how that history would become an integral part of their newborn son's personal journey. In attempting to set out some of that personal journey here, I will try to bring you to Lebanon and back.

## *Operation Litani – The Israeli Invasion of Lebanon*

By 11 March 1978, I am ten years old. I'm riding my red bicycle up and down Ballygall Avenue. I got it for Christmas. In Israel, little ten-year-old Yitzhak Ankwa, known affectionately as Yitzik, is excited. He is going with his little sister, Galit (aged two), on a bus trip along Israel's coastal highway just north of Tel Aviv.

As the Ankwa children play and fidget and gaze out of the windows in the tour bus, Dalal Mughrabi and ten other Palestinian guerrillas are rowing quietly ashore at the beach at Ma'agan Michael. Just one mile from the Israeli coastal highway north of Tel Aviv. The Popular Front for the Liberation of Palestine (PFLP) and the Palestine Liberation Organisation (PLO) had fled to Lebanon in the late 1960s and were well established in the Lebanese coastal cities of Tyre, Sidon and Beirut at the time of the Ankwa family's day trip. Mughrabi and her fellow guerrillas have reached Israeli territory from Lebanon in Zodiac rubber dinghies. They have managed to navigate the short distance south along the Mediterranean coastline undetected. Approaching the beach, they've cut the engines and are paddling gently ashore.

Gail Rubin, a forty-year-old photographer from New York is also on the beach at Ma'agan Michael. She is taking shots of wild seabirds among the marram grass. She is oblivious to the approach of the Palestinians. They splash ashore and begin unpacking and assembling their weapons. Kalashnikov assault rifles, grenades, explosives. Gail turns into the salt sea breeze of the Mediterranean and is taken by surprise as a number of figures approach her from the surf. She squints to see who else might be on the beach this early. Perhaps they are fishing.

The Palestinians approach her. And Gail knows in her heart and stomach that something is terribly wrong. They are too intense. Too close. Crowding around her and her camera equipment. At gunpoint they demand directions to Tel Aviv. She feels a surge of adrenaline. She thinks of her parents, Jonathan and Estelle, in their family home in New York. For Jonathan and Estelle it is Friday night, Eastern Standard Time. They have lit the Shabbat candles and prepare for the short Kabbalat Shabbat prayer service. They pray for their precious daughter. Their only child.

Gail focuses on the gun pointed at her. Aimed point blank towards her head. Her mind is racing. Fear, disappointment, sadness. Before she can say 'no', or 'please', there is a loud crack. Gail does not hear this sound. Only a sudden, inexplicable force which pushes her backwards and upwards. Then wet sand on her skin. Seeping cold through her clothes. The warm rush of her own blood mingling with the salt and sand. The Palestinians file past her lifeless body. Stepping around her camera equipment, they begin moving towards the coastal highway.

The Egged tour bus with Yitzik and little Galit on board suddenly slows and comes to a halt on the highway. Figures on the road waving it down. Through the window, the Ankwa children can see the glittering Mediterranean. Then, another series of loud cracking sounds. The man in front of them slumps in his seat as the Palestinians take the bus at gunpoint. The children stare at the blood sprayed all over the window and seatback.

The bus is driven south by the Palestinians. They shoot passengers in the bus. They shoot at passing cars. The children scream and weep. Parents plead. One by one, they too are shot. Including thirty-eight-year-old Haviv Ankwa. The bus is eventually halted by Israeli police at Herzliya. Thirty-eight Israelis are killed in the hijacking. Seventy-one are wounded. All of the Palestinians are killed. The Ankwa children die also.

The incident is known in Israel as the Coastal Road Massacre.

Three days later, the Israeli Defence Forces invade Lebanon in Operation Litani. They occupy the southern part of Lebanon in order to crush the PFLP and the PLO.

And two months later, in May of 1978, the first Irish troops arrive in south Lebanon as part of the United Nations Interim Force in Lebanon. They arrive as peacekeepers.

As I write, in the summer of 2012, the Irish Defence Forces are still soldiering in Lebanon. The Irish army have had an almost continuous presence in Lebanon over four decades. Over that time, many thousands of Irish soldiers have witnessed at first hand the bitter internecine violence within Lebanon. They have also witnessed the subsequent Israeli invasions of Lebanon in 1982, 1993, 1996 and 2006.

In total, Irish soldiers have served more than 40,000 individual tours of duty in Lebanon. All over Ireland, in almost every family across the country, there is an intimate link with Lebanon. An uncle, perhaps. A cousin. A niece. A son or daughter who has served in the cause of international peace. Despite this intimate linkage with the suffering of our brothers and sisters in Lebanon and Israel, there is little public understanding of our military involvement in Lebanon.

This book is intended to redress that imbalance. It takes the reader to Lebanon through the eyes of a young officer on his first tour of duty overseas. It reveals the true nature and intensity of peacekeeping operations. The book reveals for the first time what war is like for Irish soldiers serving in Irish uniform under the UN flag. It speaks frankly of the psychological stress and fear experienced by Irish troops under fire. It speaks of the squalor of modern warfare. And the suffering and pain inflicted on innocent civilians – men, women and children alike.

I served in Lebanon as an artillery officer with the 78th Irish Battalion from October 1995 to April 1996. As a lieutenant, I was Group Commander of the Dismountable Element of the Battalion Mobile Reserve (BMR). The BMR was the mobile armoured element of the Irish Battalion. It acted as the rapid reaction force of the Irish Battalion in Lebanon. It was designed to act as the '911' element of the force – the first responders to any major incident within the Irish Area of Operations (AO). These incidents ranged from intervening in and preventing the killing of innocent civilians, to armed confrontations with Hizbullah or the Israeli Defence Forces (IDF). My fellow officers in Lebanon jokingly referred to this unit as the 'Disposable Element' of the BMR because of the number of armed confrontations in which we became involved.

The account given here of my time in Lebanon is based on actual events recorded in the official Unit History of the 78th Infantry Battalion. This unit history is held at Military Archives in Cathal Brugha Barracks, Dublin. The hostile incidents and escalation of combat operations throughout south Lebanon described in this book are recorded in detail in the Unit History. The war between Hizbullah and Israel which took place in April of 1996 was eventually named Operation Grapes of Wrath by the Israeli Government of Shimon Peres. The first-hand account of Operation Grapes of Wrath given in this book is based on my own personal experiences, diaries and letters.

However, in order to protect the sensitivities of my fellow soldiers, I have changed the names, distinguishing details and characteristics of those Irish troops with whom I served in Lebanon. As a consequence, apart from myself, the soldiers described in this book are not based on any real person, living or dead. They are composite personalities. Any resemblance to the actual members of the 78th Battalion is entirely coincidental. I have employed this device out of respect for my colleagues who suffered so much – and gave so much of themselves – in the most harrowing of circumstances in Lebanon. To this end, I have endeavoured to create a narrative that protects the identities of the living and the dead alike.

I give an account of a suicide in this book. Whilst there were no suicides during the 78th Battalion's deployment, I experienced at first hand the suicide of several fellow soldiers during my military service. In addition to those killed in action in Lebanon, a small but tragic number of Irish soldiers died by suicide there. I include the account of suicide in their memory. I include it also in order to highlight the pain and suffering brought about by the growing prevalence of suicide in Irish society.

In summary, the incidents in this account of service in Lebanon are based on actual events recorded in the Unit History of the 78 Infantry Battalion, UNIFIL. However, I have used some artistic licence to protect the identities of colleagues and have, from time to time, incorporated some of the experiences of other Irish soldiers in order to give a broader focus and a more rounded feel to the book. I have done this to provide the reader with an authentic sense of what it was like to serve in the Irish army in Lebanon at that time.

It should also be noted that the account is based on my experiences of the Irish Defence Forces of the mid 1990s. The book is firmly located in that place and time. There have been many changes in the Defence Forces since then. This book is a snapshot of the past. It is an honest attempt to tell the true story of the Irish soldier in Lebanon at that stage of the Defence Forces historical development.

In attempting to contextualise my military service overseas, I have also made extensive reference to my own personal and family circumstances. I have done so in order to try and communicate a wider truth about soldiering, fatherhood, insight and loss. I refer to the personal in order to try and communicate the individual catharsis that experience of conflict can bring. For some, that catharsis brings insight into the truth of our fragile human existence. Perhaps even closure, with the ability to live a reflective and fulfilled life. For others, there is no reflection. No closure. For some soldiers, there is no way home. Some seek comfort and oblivion in alcohol or other drugs.

I tell this story in memory of all those Irish men and women who have soldiered abroad under the flag of the United Nations. In whatever army. In whatever conflict. I tell it in memory of those who never came home and who lost their lives in the cause of peace. I tell it particularly for all of us who came home altered. For tens of thousands of Irish men and women, a part of their hearts and souls remains in Lebanon.

Finally, I write this for peace. I write it in solidarity with the suffering of our brothers and sisters – Arab and Israeli alike – in Lebanon and Israel. I write it for all those innocent civilians who are caught up in the horror of modern warfare. For war is not principally a story about soldiers and guns. It is a story about the suffering of innocent men, women and children who fall victim to the tragic failures of our political leaders.

# Chapter 1

# The Leb

*Blessed are the peacemakers, for they shall be called children of God*
Matthew 5:9

'In the unlikely event of a loss of air pressure within the cabin, an oxygen mask will automatically be lowered in front of you.' October, 1995. The air hostess is just finishing the usual routine about mid-air explosions and death at 37,000 feet and so on. The Aer Lingus Airbus has already started rolling. I squeeze myself tighter into the window seat and try to get a last glimpse of Ireland. The 2 AM raindrops roll sideways across the glass.

Then, there is the roar of engines as we gather momentum and speed down the western runway. Rattling overhead bins. The banging and slapping of tires accelerating over the concrete. Two hundred and twenty men on the aircraft – the first rotation of troops – known as 'Chalk 1' heading for the Leb. There is total silence as fathers, brothers, sons, lovers, are lost in their own thoughts – thinking of loved ones sleeping below. Thinking of their own now-empty beds, hundreds of them in homes all across Ireland.

And then the aircraft lurches into the air. Climbing. I strain to catch a final sight of Dublin. And there she is. Dublinia. Aglow below me. Bathed in a sodium wash of orange streetlights. Necklaces of light strewn from the Dublin foothills towards the bay. Dense coils of light at the city centre. Then, the cloud base, grey and black. 'Good luck and fuck ye,' says Corporal B in 7A. There is a ripple of laughter. I say a silent prayer – even though I don't really believe in God – for my parents. I think of my girl-friend down there. Somewhere in the city.

It is a six-hour night flight to Beirut. But I cannot sleep. So, I wander around the gloom of the aircraft. Some of the air hostesses are engaged in whispered conversations here and there. They smile as I pass. I meet the Padre, Father Ryan, coming out of the toilet. 'First time?' he asks me. Then, leaning conspiratorially towards me, he speaks in a low voice, filled with urgency. 'Drink as much water as you can, Thomas. Beirut is hot as hell. Otherwise you'll be totally de-hydrated before we even get to the coast-road.' So I drink about three litres of water.

Some of the troops are eating oranges. Guys I don't recognise from A Company – the Dubs. Or 'The Vikings' as they are referred to in Army parlance. They are wolfing those oranges down and smiling in a slightly sinister way. We are all bound for the same destination. Post Six Four Zero – Al Yatun. As they devour the fruit, the A Company troops eye me with that peculiar mixture of contempt and curiosity which is reserved for junior officers. Especially ones they don't know. Junior officers are generally regarded by the troops as a necessary evil. At best. And at worst, a health and safety hazard.

I meet some of my own guys from the Battalion Mobile Reserve. The BMR. We are the 911 of the Battalion. I am especially proud of this status. We are a mix of cavalry and artillery – troopers and gunners – who will provide the emergency response for the entire Irish AO. When there is trouble, we'll be called out. When the shit hits the fan, we are 'operational'. I love it.

When I told my Dad this interesting fact, he let out a low whistle.

'Couldn't they get some other fuckin' eejit to do that job?' But I was ready for anything. Mexican stand-offs at checkpoints, firefights – imagine! – I was all set. I was oven ready. Thus perhaps confirming the troops' well-founded suspicion and fear of junior officers.

My Battery Sergeant, my right-hand man, approaches me. BS Begley. A Gaelgoir (native Irish speaker) from Kerry. He is built like the proverbial brick shithouse. He is very soft spoken and unusually quiet for an NCO. He has taken me under his wing and thus far managed to keep me out of trouble. For the most part. 'Relax,' he says. 'We're passing through Turkish airspace now. We'll be on the ground shortly. So if I were you I'd try to get some rest. You'll be busy enough when we get there.'

I take his advice and head back to my window seat. On the way I make eye contact with the rest of my NCOs. Sergeant Bracken nods in reassurance. A Kildare man, he has also adopted me. He has endless patience. The three corporals are watching me and grinning broadly. Corporal Kennedy from Balbriggan in Dublin is hard to read. Cold blue eyes. He hasn't said much to me since the form-up of the battalion. I'm told he's 'rock steady'. I'll find out soon enough. Corporal Burke from Donegal is highly strung. He calls out to me. 'How's about ye?' as I pass. Corporal Smith from County Meath is a young guy. Maybe twenty years old. He is reading some geeky computer magazine. He doesn't look up.

As I screw myself back into the seat, the officer next to me opens one eye. 'Where are you posted?' he enquires.

'Al Yatun.'

'I'd rather have a hot poker stuck up my arse,' is his reply as he pulls his cavalry Glengarry down over his eyes. That gives me food for thought.

*

The plane begins its descent, the Mediterranean suddenly below us as we track south over the Lebanese coastline. Flying east, the sun has risen. The sky is cobalt blue with the sea glittering below. We bank left and are descending into Beirut airport. The city is ringed to the north by mountains. It is incredibly beautiful. White apartment blocks. White villas with red-tiled roofs. Palm trees.

As we make our final approach the suburbs flash below us. Like a show reel. Swimming pools. Elaborate terraced gardens. A blur of red rooftops. Beirut. The Paris of the Middle East. The thunk of the wheels lowering. The rush of air. Then the bump and roar of airbrakes announcing our arrival.

'*Fáilte roimh go léir go dtí an Liobán*,' says the pilot.

'Fuck you too,' says Corporal B in 7A. More laughter.

Things move rapidly. The senior officers are up standing. The troops are up fumbling with the overhead bins. Like schoolboys going on a daytrip. But the nervous tension of earlier is gone. The Company Sergeant (CS) in charge of our reception – who arrived a week earlier – is the first through the aircraft door.

'EVERYONE SIT THE FUCK DOWN,' he roars. Everyone, officers included, sits down. 'EXCEPT THE OFFICERS,' he clarifies at 1,000 decibels. We stand up again. We file out.

I am squinting as we emerge into the glare of brilliant sunshine. My first impressions of Lebanon. The smell of aviation fuel. And the heat. A wall of shimmering, super heat. The Padre eyes me meaningfully as he swigs from a two litre bottle of Ballygowan. Ballygowan in Beirut. As we dismount and climb down the rickety steps, I am physically counted in-country by the Battalion's Executive Officer (EO). 'Welcome to Beirut, Thomas.' The Battalion EO is also from Dublin and gives me a wink. A friendly face. Good to have a potential ally in a senior officer at Battalion Headquarters.

There is a row of tables on the tarmac. At the first table I am greeted by the ordnance staff. 'As per Annex A, to Ordnance Guideline 1, I am required to ask you the following questions,' a staff sergeant intones. Then in rapid-fire staccato, 'Are you carryin guns, rifles, pistols or firearms of any kind including pen guns? Are you carrying plants, animals, birds or living creatures? Are you carrying poultry?' I am thinking about this when the CS interrupts from the rickety stairbridge to the plane. 'GET A FUCKING MOVE ON.' I am directed to the next table where I am given my UN identity card.

A Medical Corps Sergeant with a very unhealthy smile is carrying a Shamrock Rovers kit bag. The kind that kids carry to school. 'Aha, a Lieutenant,' he observes. He rummages in the bag and produces a set of metal discs on a cheap silver-coloured chain. 'These are your dog tags. Lieutenant Cloonan.'

'Eh, Clonan,' I correct him.

'Whatever.'

'Sir.'

'Just put it around your waist – loop it through your belt like so. You don't put it around your neck like in the movies. Cos if you get your fuckin' head blown off we'll never find them.' That made sense all right. I thanked him and wrapped the dog tags around my waist. '0.9721 LT CLONAN THOMAS BLOOD GP A'. My mother would have keeled over at this point. I made a mental note not to tell her about the dog tags. Especially the avuncular advice about getting your 'fuckin' head blown off'.

I then become aware of a crowd of soldiers off to the side in the shade of an aircraft hangar. Their uniforms are sun-bleached and they are deeply tanned. They are watching the aircraft very closely. Like vultures. Waiting for the main body of the troops to exit. I suddenly realise they are Irish soldiers. As Chalk 1 rotates into the Area of Operations, these 200 or so troops are rotating home after a seven-month tour of duty. They have had a quiet, uneventful tour. Then, as the first of our battalion begin to file off the aircraft, the outgoing group burst into a deafening roar. Cat-calls. 'I'll be ridin' yer wife this time tomorrow night ye sad bastard ye.' 'Happy fuckin' Christmas.' 'Only seven months to go – but whose fuckin' countin?' Whistling. Cheering. Clapping. Stamping. Some are banging bits of timber off the corrugated walls of the shed. The noise is deafening. One of them starts up on a bagpipes. The piper is playing 'Silent Night' at full volume. Reminding us – somewhat cruelly – where we'll be spend-ing next Christmas. There are some Lebanese workers watching intently from the shade. I imagine they find the Irish a curious lot.

In less than an hour, we are off the aircraft and sitting in a fleet of canvas-covered trucks. French army trucks. Ancient, high-axled Renaults. The outgoing, home-bound troops have boarded the Aer Lingus jet. The airbus taxis away from us in the shimmering heat. It seems to move through liquid. We watch in silence as it thunders down the run-way – heading west, climbing over the Mediterranean. Full of laughing, sweating Irish soldiers. On their way home to wives, girlfriends, families, kids. To God knows what. And we are finally, definitively, irretrievably in the Leb. 'At last,' I'm thinking, 'adventure.' I take in the guys in my truck. Good. There's Corporal Kennedy, my Dublin NCO. The rest are mainly infantry. 'The Vikings' from A Company. They are muttering muti-nously about the heat.

We wait in the trucks. The heat is searing. No movement. Hurry up and wait. In classic Army style. The CS moves up and down the vehicles.

'Our Lebanese fuckin' army fuckin' escort has not arrived. Be fuckin' patient. Believe me gentlemen, and be advised, we've all fuckin' day to get to the hills.' Then it starts.

In my truck, one of the soldiery announces, 'I'm dyin' for a piss.' This is followed by a chorus of 'Yeah, I'm dyin for a piss.' Corporal Kennedy turns towards me and stares at me with his cold, baby-killer blue eyes. 'Well?' he asks. The moment has arrived. This is my first command decision overseas. I am also at bursting point. I silently curse the Padre and stand up to issue my first order.

I am however being overtaken by events. Some of the lads are climbing down off the truck and emptying their bladders in all directions. In fact, for one moment, I'm positive that at least two are having a pissing competition to see who can pee the farthest onto the tarmac. I stand up and issue my first order in a live operational environment in the Middle East. I remember my training – CLAP: Clear, Loud, As an Order and Precise. I manage to blurt out, 'Eh, get back in the truck.' Nobody hears me.

Then, I hear the CS. 'GET BACK IN THE FUCKIN TRUCK. WHO IS IN CHARGE IN THAT TRUCK? WHO THE FUCK IS IN CHARGE OF THIS? THIS, THREE RING CIRCUS?'

The troops scatter and are calling out in unison, 'It was that Lieutenant Cloonan, CS. He told us to take a piss before we hit the road.' The CS appears at the rear of the truck. His face is red with rage. Veins bulging at his temples.

'Eh, that should be Lieutenant Clonan, not Cloonan,' I inform him.

'OK Lieutenant Cloonan. This is a fuckin' muslim country. They don't like seein' penises under any circumstances.' He is joined by a staff officer from Battalion Headquarters. Another red-faced man. I recognise him as Commandant Molloy. A 'renowned' ex-GAA 'star' and all-round golden balls. He peers in at me.

'Cloonan. I fuckin' knew it. We're only in-country one hour and you—'

Before he can finish the sentence, the trucks roar into life and we jerk forward. I am – not for the first time, and not for the last time – saved by the bell.

Our Lebanese army escorts are lethargic looking. Draped across the back of two old US jeeps, one cradles an M16. Another is leaning against a point five machine gun. It doesn't look as though it has been fired in a long time. In fact, I can see rust on the recoil mechanism from my perch in the back of the truck. Corporal Kennedy has slid down the bench and is sitting next to me. He too is squinting at the Lebanese soldiers bouncing along the pot-holed road alongside us. 'Fuckin Israelis,' he says. I am thinking of pointing out the fact that we are not in Israel when we are interrupted. One of the A Company soldiers is shouting from the other end of the truck. I can hardly hear him over the noise of the engine and the flapping of the canvas cover. I can't see him either over the mountain of kit bags and boxes piled high in the bed of the truck. 'What's your nickname sir?' is what I can make out. They are all laughing now and I don't like the liberal atmosphere I detect among the infantry. Or the 'infantiles' as they are referred to by the Artillery Corps.

Corporal Kennedy leans in and whispers urgently in my ear. 'Fuckin' ignore them A Company heads.' I, however, have decided to finally, once and for all, take control of this truck. I stand up and grip the overhead bar. As the truck bumps and sways over the potholes, I declare in a voice that everyone can hear, 'Listen up ladies, I don't have a nickname. But you can call me sir. Is that clear?' There is an instant round of applause and, feeling pleased with myself, I sit down again. Corporal Kennedy is shaking his head. The next thing I hear is a disembodied voice shout, 'Shithead. That's his nickname. Shithead.' There is more laughter.

Corporal Kennedy looks at me point blank. 'I told ya not to say anything, didn't I? They don't call them the 'empty-heads' for nuthin'. Let me look after it. Sir.' Corporal Kennedy then slides off the bench and disappears into the throng. All hell breaks loose. I hear a loud series of thumping noises.

Eventually, Corporal Kennedy re-emerges. Smiling beatifically. 'They have decided not to proceed with nicknames,' he announces. Alarmed, I ask him if he's assaulted anyone in A Company. He cocks his head sideways. 'Praise where praise is due, and management where it isn't. Do they not teach you that in officer school?'

Meanwhile the southern suburbs of Haret Chbib and Dawha are receding behind us. All along the coast road we see men walking hand in hand. The troops find this endlessly amusing. Everyone we see is smoking. Boys selling fish from wooden crates. Smoking. Soldiers everywhere. Smoking. Some with black berets. Some with red berets. Some on motorbikes. Some in pairs on motorbikes sitting side-saddle. All smoking. And everywhere there is rubble. No building seems complete. Bullet holes and crumbling plasterwork on every façade. The streetscape is an unending crazy maze of ramshackle buildings. Children are running alongside the vehicles. The troops are throwing whatever food they have out to them. Bottles of Ballygowan. Yoghurts. Apples. Chocolate. Everything except the oranges.

And everywhere there are wires looped around poles, trees, draped from buildings. There is no order. No regular or predictable urban feature. Sudden gaps between the houses where bomb craters lie. Collapsed bridges. Flattened cars. Every so often the brains, spines and entrails of sheep, cows and goats are displayed proudly on metal hooks beside doorways. Great clouds of blue flies swept away from the meat on display by small boys. Women dressed in black glare at us from doorways and windows. We pass by a wooden shack on the side of the road. A painted sign reads 'Al Pacino Chiken'. Corporal Kennedy spies it. 'We must stop in that gaff and try the Al Pacino chicken thing out. Next time we're doin convoy security up to Beirut.' I look at him. He is serious.

As we approach the coastal city of Sidon, the motorway opens up. We pick up speed. Two of the A Company soldiers are puking over the tail-gate. I'm told that the oranges were full of vodka. Apparently, the infantry guys had a paramedic with them in Dublin who injected the fruit with vodka. Some of the guys are more than half cut.

We drive through Sidon. The trucks slow to a crawl once more. Lebanese men in ancient Mercedes honking incessantly on their horns. Tens of thousands of mercs driven by men with moustaches. Again, all smoking. The noise is incredible. There are no apparent rules of the road. Some of the younger Lebanese guys are driving tarted up mercs along what I assume is the footpath. Every now and again we skirt around a car driving the opposite way through the throng. Drivers and passengers shaking their fists at all and sundry. Arabic music blasts in and out of the truck from passing cars, from windows and from ghetto blasters on the outdoor stalls. Eventually we exit south from Sidon's crammed streets and pass what looks like a vast municipal dump on the side of a hill. On closer inspection however, the 'dump' turns out to be a Palestinian refugee camp. Millions of Palestinians live in abject poverty within Lebanon. Treated like second-class citizens, they are forced to eke out a miserable existence in camps such as this throughout the country.

We hear a popping sound. Like bangers at Halloween. The trucks accelerate. Everyone is now lying on the floor of the truck. We are being fired at from the refugee camp. Corporal Kennedy is grinning at me. 'They fuckin' hate the Lebbos. But they fuckin' hate the UN even more.'

Our convoy comes to a halt in the late afternoon not far from the coastal city of Tyre. We have arrived at the River Litani. The Litani is the gateway to South Lebanon. We dismount from the trucks and stretch our legs. It is like a scene from the catechism books I had in primary school. The Litani flows gently along grassy banks lined with palm trees, olive groves and vines. Even lemon and orange trees. The troops are now urinating en masse into the Litani. I join them.

'STOP PISSING IN THE LITANI! IT'S A FUCKIN' SACRED RIVER FOR GOD'S SAKE!' The CS has re-appeared. We are ordered to put on flak jackets as we have officially entered the free-fire zone.

I am called away by the Battalion Executive Officer. He spreads a map over the bonnet of a white UN four-wheel drive. 'OK Thomas, this is where we were fired on.' He marks the map with a red military symbol and hands it to me. 'When you are commanding the convoy security next week, remember to navigate away from this area. Maybe you ought to get out here and recce the route.' I appreciate the kindness of Commandant Evans. I also appreciate his confidence in me.

When I get back to the vehicle lines, the BMR is now being shaken out by BS Begley. I'm the last to get to the flak jackets and helmets. The flak jacket I get has no ballistic plates. They've been long lost, or stolen or sold or who knows. My blue helmet has a skull and crossbones crudely drawn on the front. 'Born to Die' is scrawled under it in black permanent marker. 'Cool helmet, Sir.' Corporal Smith has abandoned his computer magazine and is examining the radio frequencies provided by the outgoing BMR signals team. We have now entered the Area of Operations.

# Chapter 2

# Irishbatt

*Your Lebanon is an arena for men from the West and men from the East.*
*My Lebanon is a flock of birds fluttering in the early morning as shepherds*
*lead their sheep into the meadow and rising in the evening as farmers return*
*from their fields and vineyards.*

Kahlil Gibran, *Mirrors of the Soul*

Our stop at the Litani allows us to impose some semblance of order on the troops. Our 'Order of March' or OOM is now organised along a unit by unit basis. With the Battalion Mobile Reserve split into two – a vehicle at the front and rear of the column – we begin to trundle south from the Litani towards Tyre. From there, we will head east, inland towards the Irish AO.

The terrain is spectacular. Tyre is home to the coliseum where Charlton Heston races his chariot in the movie *Ben Hur*. As we move east the old town gives way to more ramshackle suburbs. Houses are built to a height of two or three storeys and appear mostly unfinished. They are concrete and stone affairs with rough sand and cement dashing. The roofs are flat with twisting metal and iron girders protruding from the rough concrete finish. BS Begley – this is his fourth tour of duty in Lebanon – explains to me that the upper floors will be built upon as finances allow and as more members of the extended family join the original inhabitants. 'They'll extend out and up to house their children and their wives and families. Whole family groups or clans live in extended houses.' Children are running alongside the convoy. We've run out of food to throw to them. The troops wave. The kids are laughing and shouting in Arabic.

Dotted among the houses are massive red-tiled villas on their own grounds. Surrounded by elaborate terraced gardens. Some have lawns with sprinklers. Most are gated with electronic monitoring systems, CCTV cameras, buzzers and intercoms. According to BS Begley, these houses belong to local 'notables' – *daoine mór le rá* – such as doctors, politicians and businessmen. Many are empty for much of the year. A lot of the Lebanese – similar to the Irish – emigrate to the US, Africa, Asia or further afield in the Middle East to avail of opportunities outside of war-torn Lebanon. The Lebanese, I will discover, are natural raconteurs and communicators. And, like the Irish, they are warm and friendly – charming, but also deeply passionate about their country, culture and history. For millennia, Lebanon, with its Mediterranean coastline, has been an important trading post between Asia and Europe. Beirut, like Damascus in neighbouring Syria, is on the ancient Silk Route. As a consequence, perhaps, they are intensely interested in foreigners. They are highly skilled in reading character and establishing common ground. It seems to me a tragedy that they are locked in conflict with Israel.

As the convoy moves east from Tyre we begin to ascend gradually. The roads are narrow as we climb hundreds of metres into a complex series of ridgelines and wadi systems. As the sun begins to set, the rock glows a spectacular red and burnt orange in all directions. The blue sky is edged with pink just over the shimmering horizon. I notice the sheer drops on either side of the switchbacks as we pass through Qana – where 'allegedly', as Corporal Kennedy tells me, 'Jesus turned the water into wine' – and Deir Ntar. At As Sultaniyah, the convoy is met by armoured personnel carriers from the outgoing Irish Battalion. They escort us to Tibnine. We pass through the first Irish checkpoints. We are now officially at home in the Irish Battalion Area of Operatons – or 'Irishbatt AO' for short. The soon-to-depart Irish troops are happy to see us arrive. They cat-call continuously. The air turns blue as we enter Camp Shamrock. What remains of Headquarters Company greet their replacements with malicious glee.

We have now arrived at our penultimate destination. Camp Shamrock is the administrative and logistics centre of Irishbatt AO. Irishbatt AO is roughly 100 square kilometres in size, and forms the south-eastern flank of the overall United Nations Interim Force in Lebanon (UNIFIL) deployment. The Irish patrol and occupy an area that stretches from Kiryat Shmona in northern Israel to the Israeli-Lebanese border town of Rosh Hanikra on the Mediterranean coastline. This mountainous area – known as 'the Hills' by Irish troops – contains just over a dozen towns. Some of the names are familiar to Irish people. Villages such as Tibnin, Brashit, At-Tiri and Bayt Yahun. Dozens of Irish troops have been killed in action in these villages – far away from home and loved ones. Many hundreds of others have had epiphanies – serious injuries and other life-changing experiences – within the confines and outskirts of these Arab villages. I and my unlikely comrades in A Company and the BMR will soon be a part of that collective – and relatively unspoken – Irish experience.

The Irishbatt towns and villages are more or less controlled by Hizbullah. As such, the Irishbatt AO is a flashpoint area. It is especially volatile given the fact that the Israeli-Lebanese border itself lies within the AO. Matters in Irishbatt are further complicated by the ongoing presence of the Israeli Defence Forces (IDF) within the area. The

Lebanese-Israeli Armistice Demarcation Line or ADL runs straight through the Irish AO with a frontage of 22km. The Israelis have created a buffer zone on Lebanese soil along this front. It is a de facto occupied zone. A free fire zone – with often horrific consequences for all those unfortunate enough to live there. Or, from time to time, for those who are deployed there as peacekeepers.

In effect, approximately half of the Irish Area of Operations is occupied by the IDF. The IDF occupy a series of hill-top fortifications and firebases throughout the AO. They reinforce their positions and patrols with their local proxies in Lebanon, the South Lebanon Army (SLA). This portion of the Irish AO is known as the ICA or Israeli Controlled Area. It is along this fault-line between the Israeli Controlled Area and the Hizbullah heartland that Irishbatt suffers most of its casualties. In fact, approximately half of Irishbatt's casualties have been inflicted by Hizbullah and other Arab resistance movements. The other half have been inflicted by the IDF and SLA. We are, as BS Begley remarks, 'Piggy in the middle.'

Camp Shamrock, or Position 6-43, is located on the rear slope of the ridgeline running just behind the town of Tibnine. This is Battalion Headquarters – housing the Headquarters Company, the unit that provides support to the remainder of the Irish Battalion in the form of Transport, Logistics, Administration – including discipline and courts martial – Signals, Medical, Engineering and Explosive Ordnance Disposal (EOD) Platoons. Camp Shamrock is also the home of the Battalion Commander and his Staff Officers. It is a place to be avoided by junior officers – if at all possible.

The remainder of the Irish Battalion is made up of 500 or so men and women divided up into three main companies. The bulk of the troops are infantry and form A, B and C Companies. A Company is headquartered in Al Yatun, near the village of Haris. A Company – which comprises troops from Dublin – occupies a string of villages from Haris, through Tibnine to position 6-5 or 'Fraggle Rock' near Majdal Silm in the Northeast.

B Company Headquarters is located at position 6-38 in Haddatha. B Company's troops are drawn from Munster and in the towns of Bayt Yahun, Ayta Zutt and elsewhere, locals and soldiers alike speak English with pronounced Cork, Kerry and Limerick accents. B Company holds the towns and villages to the southwest of the Irishbatt AO from Rshaf and At Tiri up to Ash Sha'fa.

C Company Headquarters is based at position 6-16 in Brashit. C Company consists of troops primarily drawn from the Donegal and Connemara Gaeltacht. There are a smattering of troops also from some border units and the midlands. As a consequence, the Arab traders or 'Mingy Men' from Brashit to Shaqra speak English with a northern twang. Often they have a *cúpla focail gaeilge*.

We are tired and thirsty when we arrive in Shamrock. We've been travelling now for almost twenty-four hours.

'A COMPANY AND BMR – GET THE FUCK OUT OF MY CAMP,' the BMR and A Company personnel are directed by the rotation CS in his unique and inimitable fashion to Post 6-40 at Al Yatun. Just minutes from Tibnine, Al Yatun – my home for the next seven months – is situated on the highest point of the ridgeline that dominates the northern sector of the Irish Area of Operations.

As we head up the hill towards Al Yatun, I scan the map. I see the names of villages that I will become intimately acquainted with. Villages such as Rshaf, Bayt Yahun, Shaqrah, Jumay Jumay, Majdal Silm. Like the Sorrowful Mysteries, I will recite them in my mind for decades to come.

# Chapter 3

# Al Yatun

*Watch out for the scorpions. They like to hide in your desert boots.*
*Or worse, if they get inside the mosquito net.*

Al Yatun – or Hill 679 – is now home. Escorted by the Armoured Personnel Carriers (APCs) of the BMR, we swing through the fortified, sandbagged entrance. 'Here we are – Al Ya Fuckin' Gloom,' remarks Corporal Kennedy. 'On good days, we call it Al Ya Fun. Eh, but mostly Al Ya Gloom. If you get me drift, Sir.'

I'm taking it in as best I can. Post 6-40 is about the size of a football pitch. It is surrounded by blast walls, stone gabions and barbed wire. There is a machine gun post overlooking the checkpoint at the entrance. There is another machine gun mounted in the observation post located at the rear perimeter of our position. There are approximately 120 men in the post. The troops are housed in a series of single-storey portakabins. There are a few shower blocks with toilet and washing facilities. There is also a cook-house and a canteen where – remarkably – troops who are not on duty or on patrol can buy bottles of Almaza, the local Lebanese beer. There is a great deal of noise coming from the canteen. It sounds like someone is being murdered in slow motion. 'Don't ever go in there on your own, Sir,' whispers BS Begley.

The position is built around an old Lebanese villa. This has long since been converted into the communications centre and operations room for A Company and the BMR. The remaining rooms in the villa comprise the officer's mess, with a dining room and a bar. I use the term officer's mess in the loosest manner. Its biggest advantage it seems is that it has thick walls – 'capable of stopping a high velocity round' according to 'Psycho' Dunne, the Communications Centre NCO and public address announcer for Al Yatun. There are plenty of pock marks in the walls to attest to this particular health and safety characteristic. BS Begley dismounts and swings his kitbag over his shoulder. He summons Sergeant Bracken and the corporals for their operational handover in the communications centre.

I join the other officers for our own handover in the Operations (Ops) briefing room. My predecessor, another artillery officer, will be flying home on the next Chalk. I've got one week to pick his brains before I assume full operational command of my own troops. Seven days to familiarise myself with all of the patrol routes within the Irishbatt AO. Seven days to identify all of the main players within our area, from village Muktars (mayors) to Lebanese Army officers, interpreters, local Mingy Men (traders), Imams, spies on either side and of course the local Hizbullah and IDF 'players'. If not meeting them in person, then learning about them by reputation.

There is a long list of names. Captain Said Serhan is the Lebanese Intelligence Officer in Tibnine. The military leader of AMAL – an Islamic resistance group with twenty-two seats in Parliament – is Haj Abu Yasser. Hizbullah's military leader is guided by Sheikh Nasrallah, who has recently directed that their 128 members of parliament withdraw cooperation and support for the Lebanese government. Hizbullah have also demonstrated an improving ability to mount sophisticated attacks on the Israeli hilltop positions. The signs are that the situation may deteriorate. Or as A Company's Operations Officer put it – rather too cheerfully – 'As the song goes gentlemen, there may be trouble ahead. So, be ready to face the music.' The outgoing officers are elated. They've had an uneventful summer tour of duty – from April to October. They are happy to leave the winter tour, from October to next April, and the trouble that is brewing on the horizon, to us.

We are issued with our weapons. We will be armed 24/7 for the next seven months. I am issued with a Browning automatic pistol with eighteen rounds of 9mm ammunition. In addition, BS Begley insists that I'm also issued with the standard Steyr assault rifle with ninety rounds of 5.56mm ammunition. 'That pistol is about as useful as wheels on a tomato,' he remarks. 'Better to have a rifle for the stand-offs. *Na daoine uaisle* [the gentle folk] of the Hizbullah tend to notice them a bit more.' I familiarise my troops with the underground bunkers – in case of shelling or air strike – and go through the readiness alerts, code words and signals with each man.

My predecessor, Lieutenant Murphy – or 'Spud' Murphy – is about six foot two. An accomplished GAA player, he is anxious to return to club and county football when he returns to Ireland. He has a dark sense of humour and delivers his entire handover to me in GAA parlance. He describes the ring of Israeli hilltop positions as 'IDF full-forwards marking the local Hizbullah.' He tells me that at the moment – in terms of killings – it is a 'draw' between the IDF, SLA and Hizbullah. He warns me, though, that for Hizbullah 'It's all to play for' in the coming, darkening months. He also tells me that according to the intelligence estimate – based on an analysis of Hizbullah's evolving tactics and strategy – that the long dark evenings following Ramadan will herald a renewed assault on the IDF in Irishbatt's AO. 'If it kicks off anywhere, it'll kick off here.' The outgoing Ops Officer tells us that 'The shit is very definitely about to hit the fan.' None of which is at all reassuring.

Lieutenant Murphy shows me the BMR officer's billet. It is a small portakabin with two beds, two lockers and two tables. The beds are covered with mosquito nets. There is a small diesel fuel 'Damascus Heater' attached to the wall. He warns me to 'Watch out for the scorpions. They like to hide in your desert boots. Or worse, if they get inside the mosquito net.' The outgoing Cavalry Officer is sleeping in the other bed. I get to sleep on the floor for the first week.

Later that night, we are invited by the NCOs of A Company and the BMR for a drink in the canteen. Spirits are high as the 'old sweats' of the outgoing A Company give the newcomers a hard time. Particularly the young soldiers. Particularly those on their first trip overseas. One private who looks about sixteen years old has attracted the unwelcome attention of a couple of hardy annuals from the weapons platoon. Their tattoos and deeply sunburned faces – heightened by years of drink – contrast with his seemingly innocent face. 'I'm as fuckin' mad as any of youse,' I hear him say. They laugh in mock amusement. The young guy stands up suddenly. The entire room goes silent. The only noise now is the loud buzzing of a huge moth that is whirring and fluttering around the exit light over their heads.

The young guy reaches up and grabs the moth. It is almost as big as a sparrow and even from where I'm standing at the other side of the room I can see the coloured lights of the bar reflected in the inky black of its huge compound eyes.

'What are you gonna fuckin do with that mot?' asks one of the guys hysterically.

'I'm gonna fuckin' eat him. That's how fuckin' mad I am.' To an enthusiastic round of applause, the young soldier then places the moth into his mouth and chews furiously. A shout of 'Swallow the fucker' is taken up with a chant of 'Swallow the mot, swallow the mot.' Eventually the youth – now purple-faced – swallows hard. He dry retches and spits to roars of approval. All that remains of the moth are the dusty traces of its colouring around his lips. His tormentors are shaking hands with him and back-slapping him. He is now officially christened 'Mad Bastard'. Even the normally taciturn Corporal Kennedy is impressed. 'Now, he *is* a mad bastard.' BS Begley looks at me. 'Didn't I tell you never to come in here on your own.' My first night in Lebanon ends in laughter. I head back to the billet. In the gloom, I see two rifles lying up against the desk. And a shotgun laid carefully across the table top. I'm sleeping in a filthy shack filled with weapons. I think of my Mum saying the Rosary. I pick my spot on the filthy floor and lie down on my issue sleeping bag. That night, on that floor, between the loud snores of the outgoing Cavalry Officer, I dream of scorpions.

# Chapter 4

# How Did I Get Here?

*You may find yourself living in a shotgun shack, You may find yourself in another part of the world . . . You may ask yourself, well, How did I get here?*
'Once in a Lifetime', The Talking Heads

How did I end up in Lebanon? How indeed. I was born on Friday, 26 August 1966. There were lots of other boys and girls born that Friday. Little Avner Ben-Gal, for example. Born in Ashkelon, Israel that same day. Little did either of us wee men know how our lives would intersect three decades later. In the Holy Land, in Jerusalem to be precise – where I would find myself standing, rooted to the spot in front of one of Ben-Gal's paintings.

I was born on a Friday. A good start. For apparently Friday's child is loving and giving. Certainly, I was much loved. My parents gave me every opportunity in life. They belonged to that generation of Irish who believed passionately in education. They encouraged all of us to make the most of school and to go to university. 'To realise your fullest potential,' as my father used to say, or rather, shout. My Grandfather, Joe Clonan, was also a policeman. After fighting in the War of Independence, he joined the newly formed Garda Síochána in the early 1920s. He was based in Kevin Street Garda Station in Dublin. Like my father, he was a hard man. He was a distant figure to me as a child. Tall. Dark haired. And to me, as a little boy – ever so slightly spoiled by my Mum – both he and my Dad seemed severe.

My Grandmother on my Mum's side was from Killorglin in Kerry. My great-grandfather, a Begley, was a teacher and founder member of the Laune Rangers GAA club. My grandmother, Mairead Begley, went to Dublin in 1916 to train as a primary school teacher. She joined Cumann na mBan and fought in the War of Independence. She then taught with Louise Gavan Duffy in Scoil Bhríde, Earlsfort Terrace and later, Ranelagh. She, like my Mum, doted on me somewhat. She told me all about the War of Independence and her adventures there. And she warned me about '*an sean namhad*,' or 'the old enemy,' England.

So. Despite all those years of schooling. Despite completing a degree in Trinity College, I eventually joined the army. And you probably don't have to be Sigmund Freud to work out why.

My education began in September 1970. September 1970 would become known throughout the Middle East as the 'era of regrettable events'. At the time, I regarded my first day of school in Finglas as a fairly regrettable event. As I trooped into my new classroom with all of the other junior infants that day, Palestinian militants were busy hijacking aircraft all over Europe. In the time it took us to hang up our coats in the Junior Infants cloakroom, the Palestinians were flying those passenger jets to Dawson's Field in Zarka, Jordan. A few days later, the Palestinians blew up the aircraft. In response, the enraged Jordanian authorities launched a series of attacks on Palestinian strongholds and enclaves. This campaign of violence became known throughout the Middle East as Black September. The events of Black September drove tens of thousands of Palestinians into forced exile in South Lebanon.

Meanwhile, we little boys lined up in Ms O'Reilly's class in St Canice's in Finglas. Each of us calling out '*anseo*' or 'present' when our names were called.

The school was a squat single-storey building on Ballygall Road West, near Finglas village. A new build of blue-grey bricks and blue wooden fascia. My first introduction to a 'hostile environment'. As my Mum coaxed me in the door of the classroom, she promised me that she'd wait there for me in the cloakroom. The teacher shepherded me into a seat next to a boy whose upper lip was curled upwards at one end in a permanent sneering, snarling scowl. Scary. His name was Tommy Quinn. And he was the bouldest boy in the class. I clearly recall another boy weeping uncontrollably on the other side of him. But I was OK. My Mum was in the cloakroom. This reassurance had given me the courage to boldly go where I had never gone before.

Tommy Quinn studied me carefully. He then picked his nose and theatrically wiped it on my jumper. My three sisters had never done that to me. My brother had never done that to me. This was a brand new experience. An introduction to the world beyond our home in Ballygall Avenue. These were new words on my page, so to speak. I contemplated this angry boy with the flashing brown eyes and the snarling lip sitting next to me – staring at me defiantly. Daring me to react. I ran for the door. The first of many escapes from school.

I fled into the cloakroom – smelling faintly of stale urine, sour milk and wet duffle coats. My Mum was gone, however. Long gone. My turn to weep uncontrollably.

And that September, as my own little drama was playing out, thousands of Palestinians were fleeing into exile in Lebanon. Little did I know – in that smelly cloakroom in Junior Infants in Finglas in September 1970 – that I too was ultimately bound for Lebanon. As were several other little boys in junior infants – including the boy who had wiped his snot on my jumper.

I got to know Tommy Quinn over the following weeks. And, as bould boys go – Tommy Quinn was fairly bould all right. For example, at age four, he single-handedly introduced the entire class to a unique form of Russian Roulette involving the local clergy. Father Andrews was our school chaplain. He wore a distinctive bowler hat. That's what I remember. And he would occasionally visit our classroom. The teacher would leave the room. Silence descending, Father Andrews would place his bowler hat on the nature table and pace up and down the rows of desks firing out questions on catechism.

If you answered incorrectly, you received a nasty poke with his index finger on the back of the head. But Tommy Quinn introduced a new element to Father Andrews's ritual – taking us to new levels of fear. As Father Andrews paced the room, Tommy would reach over to the nature table and pass the bowler hat under the tables from boy to boy. As we fumbled nervously under Tommy's hostile gaze, we each had to spit into the hat.

If you didn't spit in the hat, Tommy Quinn would knock forty shades of shite out of you during the break. If you were caught spitting into the hat, Father Andrews would surely knock forty shades of shite out of you right then and there. At age four, I had not yet heard of the expression 'Catch 22' or 'caught between a rock and a hard place'. It was however, a peculiarly apt life lesson for things to come.

I never got caught with the hat. Because, like a good little Catholic boy, I prayed – albeit in my newly acquired Finglas vernacular. 'Please Jesus, don't let me get fucking caught – please please. Thanks. Amen.'

The teachers in St Canice's worked miracles with me and my unruly classmates. Mr Hughes, the principal, was a kindly man from the border counties. '*Is mise* Aodh Mac Aodh,' (My name is Hughie Hughes) he'd proudly announce. He believed that every single one of us – regardless of address, family background or academic ability – had individual talents that needed to be discovered, encouraged and nurtured. We flourished.

My favourite teacher was Mr Moynihan from Cork. We thought he was cool because he had a big beard and long hair. He also wore flared jeans. He opened our eyes to the wide world beyond that crowded class-room on Ballygall Road West. '*Lámha Trasna*,' roughly translated as 'Fold your arms and listen', and suddenly we'd be on an ice floe high in the Arctic Circle. Or wandering through the senate in ancient Greece or Rome. He taught us by effortlessly harnessing our fertile imaginations. He opened us up to the endless possibilities residing within ourselves. Crucially, he'd get us to role play – to pretend we were great figures from world history. One day we were Roman Emperors. The next, the 1916 leaders. He got us to write letters from the Roman Senate, or Kilmainham Gaol. I vividly remember Tommy Quinn's take on Padraig Pearse. 'Dear Ma. They're goin to shoot me. The bastards.' A short but pithy summary of Irish republican history. Mr Moynihan made us proud of ourselves.

# Chapter 5

# Saved by an Accordion

*What's in the fuckin box?*

And if school wasn't challenging enough, my Mum decided it would be a good idea if I went to piano lessons with my two older sisters. The music teacher was what we'd term in St Canice's a 'starey oul wan'. She stared at me for sure. Wondering perhaps what precisely this freckle-faced boy with unkempt hair, scabby knees and muck under his fingernails was doing in her front parlour in front of her precious upright piano. My sisters, pig-tailed – and as poised as Siamese cats – executed finger exercises with precision. I watched from an overstuffed sofa covered in lace doilies and cushions. Then it was my turn.

The dreaded piano teacher lady hovered behind me. Holding a wooden twelve-inch wooden ruler like a samurai. Watching me like a hawk and taut as a bowstring she screeched instructions at me. My fingers, clunking the wrong notes. Spectacularly off key. Each time I hit a bum note, she'd thwack my knuckles with the sharp edge of the ruler. 'Ouch.' Sometimes, she'd get me across the finger nails. 'Ouch' again. All the while, my sisters would watch from the couch. Each time I got a belt of the ruler, they'd stick out their tongues at me. They seemed to enjoy this crude form of entertainment far more than any of the endless games of dolls that I was press-ganged into playing at home.

Eventually, I put my foot down. 'I'm not going to that lady to play the piano,' I announced.

'Why not?' enquired my mother.

'Because, she's a witch.'

A week later, I was on the 19A bus into town with Mum. She brought me into Walton's music shop on North Frederick Street, just short of Parnell Square and O'Connell Street. 'Now, my love,' she soothed, 'pick any musical instrument you like.' Reassured that the aforementioned witch's expertise did not extend beyond pianos, I gazed around in wonder at the musical instruments on display. Violins, cellos, guitars, drums, flutes, trumpets. There was an endless display of highly polished wood and gleaming silver. On shelves up to the ceilings. In display cases. Spread over tables. Sunlight glinting off acres of varnished timber and elegant golden fretwork. There was to be no escape from the world of music, staves and wooden rulers. 'Ouch.' And then I saw it.

Hanging from the ceiling. A 48 bass piano accordion. A Hohner. Made in Germany. High gloss red and black lacquer, gold filigree and shining black and white keys – like a piano you could hide in a box. I didn't know what in God's name I was looking at. The bellows – which remorselessly pinch the knees of small boys forced to wear shorts – looked a bit menacing. 'I'll have that yoke,' I cried. My Mum, slightly taken aback, was as good as her word. And in fairness to her, within a month or so, she had identified a piano accordion teacher prepared to take me on.

Mr Murphy taught me in a room on the third floor of a run-down Georgian house on North Great George's Street. In front of a portable Calor Kozangas gas fire, he taught me the scales and bass notes. Soft tones and vibrato. Major and minor. He was a saint. How he put up with this most incompetent student, I'll never know. What I liked about the accordion was the sheer volume that could be generated by simply pushing hard on the bellows. 'Easy now Thomas,' he'd say to me as neighbours would hammer on the walls and ceiling. 'Turn them fuckin bagpipes off,' I'd hear through mouldy wallpaper and flaking plaster partitions. This was a lot more fun than the piano.

Mr Murphy instructed me for about four years. In that time, he taught me 'Three Blind Mice', 'The Emperor Waltz' and 'Marche Slave'. No jigs, or reels or Irish traditional music. Just three songs. My personal favourite was 'Marche Slave'. I'd play it at home – melodramatically slow – to reflect my mood on contemplating school and the other crises that confronted me on a daily basis. For relatives who called, I would only play with my back to them – checking over my shoulder every now and again to ensure that no one was laughing. I recall stony-faced aunts and uncles. Poker-faced, enduring 'The Emperor Waltz' played in stop-start time. And behind them – beaming – my mother. My father, staring at me through a blue haze of cigarette smoke.

I never learned to play by ear. I had to have the music propped up on the accordion case in front of me. This fact alone was the cause of a most fortuitous outcome during my first public performance in Dublin. Because, a short while later, Mum decided that it would be a good idea if I went to Mr Murphy's music lessons on my own. So, with the accordion in its case strapped onto my Nana's shopping trolley, I was dispatched weekly into town on the 19 or 19A. This was also fun. I would buy Kojak lollypops in Colls newsagent along with apple drops and Kola Kubes. The roof of my mouth would be red-raw from sucking them by the time I got to North Great George's Street.

Then, one March evening in 1978 – just after the clock had gone forward – I got off the bus at Ballygall Road and encountered Tommy Quinn and two other desperadoes from St Canice's who were known as Byrno and Wacker. They were older than Tommy and one had a black eye. In fact, truth be told, they looked like three Mexican banditos from one of the spaghetti westerns that were big at the time. Even though there were no sound effects – no Mariachi trumpets reaching a crescendo, no mouth organ solo – I knew I was in big, big trouble.

They blocked my path. Tommy Quinn opened the stand-off. 'Well, well, well. What the fuck do we have here? If it isn't Clonan and his Ma's fuckin shoppin bag.' At that point, I ventured that it wasn't in fact 'me Ma's shopping', but in fact a '48 Bass Piano Accordion'. Indeed.

Time froze. The three amigos looked at each other in some puzzlement at this new and unforeseen development.

'And what the fuck is a forty-gate piano thing?' enquired Tommy.

'Yeah,' chimed in the chorus. 'What's in the fuckin box?' Tommy Quinn kicked at the elasticated bungee that held the whole accordion/shopping trolley contraption together. Putting his hand on my chest, he pushed me back and reached down to examine the accordion case. He fiddled with the hasps until they sprang open with a thump. He stepped back – like an American cop who has sprung the trunk of a suspicious Cadillac out on Highway 55. 'You open it,' he ordered. Resigned to my fate – which would inevitably involve some ritual humiliation and getting the shite kicked out of me – I opened the box and heaved out the accordion. I heard a low whistle behind me and a rough voice say – 'Wha in the name of Jazes is that yoke?'

Tommy Quinn's demeanour changed yet again. He walked around me in a circle. All the while eyeing the accordion with barely concealed wonder. Eventually, he reached a verdict. 'Play us a fuckin tune ye little bollicks,' he demanded. In blind panic, I prevaricated and informed my tormentors that I could not play without the sheet music. Tommy Quinn replied, 'All right, all right, keep your fuckin' hair on.' 'Byrno' was detailed to 'hold up the fuckin music.' And in a moment of magnanimity – a trait I have since learned is common to many sociopaths – Tommy Quinn motioned for me to sit on the accordion box which he had arranged on its side as a wobbly stool of sorts.

As a pre-cursor to a beating – I decided to play 'Marche Slave'. I gave it absolute socks. Dramatic pauses and plaintive minor bass. Tchaikovsky would have been pleased. There was total silence. The boys looked at each other and then at me.

'That was too fuckin sad. Play somethin else or I'll fuckin burst ye.'

So, I played 'Emperor Waltz'. Now that they enjoyed. 'That was fuckin deadly.' Tommy seemed especially pleased. 'Play another one and we'll let you off with a slap on the head.' Music to my ears. I played 'Three Blind Mice' with all of the passion I could muster. 'I fuckin know that one!' roared Tommy – his eyes flashing with pleasure and recognition. Byrno's mouth hung open in wonder – a gob of spit drooling down onto the music. 'Wacker' stood silent. Tommy Quinn – good as his word – cuffed me slightly about the head, helped me gather up the music and assisted in the re-jigging of the accordion/shopping trolley assembly. And after that – no one ever hit me in school again. Tommy Quinn saw to that.

Saved by an accordion. Who'd have thought?

# Chapter 6

# Natural Justice

*Thank you Brother O'Connor, wherever you are.*

In addition to school and the music lessons, my intellectual and social development in Finglas continued apace with the acquisition of a pair of breeding pigeons. We already had a canary called Tweety. It seemed a natural, if not inevitable, progression for a boy from Finglas to venture into the world of pigeon breeding. My Dad came off duty in Pearse Street Garda station one afternoon with a cardboard box containing two pigeons. Of a type known colloquially in Dublin as Tumblers. Mr Pigeon and Mrs Pigeon was what I called them. The experience of keeping pigeons would prompt in me what my father would later term 'a heightened sense of justice'. He'd later advise me that 'Having any sense of moral or social justice in Ireland will lead to a permanent persecution complex.' That latter observation would certainly hold true with experience. But my first encounter with the drama of natural justice arose after the pigeons kicked an egg from the nest.

Mum and I rescued it from the straw in the pigeon's hutch and placed it carefully into the oven. It hatched overnight – and the pigeons accepted the chick. I carefully supplemented the chick's diet with a mixture of warm milk and bread. He thrived. Baby Pigeon, I called him.

It became apparent however that his legs were malformed. Perhaps the reason why his parents had jettisoned the egg in the first place. Some innate, hardwired awareness in their bird brains that told them there was something wrong.

But as a superior mammal with opposable thumbs, I decided to intervene in the natural order. And, as an eight-year-old naturalist and champion of the oppressed, I hand-fed Baby Pigeon until his 'cheep cheep' was replaced with regular pigeon coo-ing and his shrivelled little body was covered in shining white feathers. But his malformed legs stuck out at right angles to his body. A peculiar little scrap, he just sat in the corner of the hutch.

That's when I read the article in the *Reader's Digest* about the 'Miracle Surgeon' who helped disabled children to walk in the favellas and shanty towns of South America. According to the *Readers Digest*, he did this by manipulating their limbs and performing miracle surgery with a penknife and other kitchen utensils. I got it into my head that somewhere in Dublin, a 'Miracle Vet' would rotate Baby Pigeon's legs somehow – clicking them miraculously into the correct position. Mum told me that the Blue Cross Van called to Finglas every fortnight or so and that I could bring Baby Pigeon to see the vet when it next arrived.

And so, on the appointed evening, I carefully cleaned Baby Pigeon and placed him gently into a shoe box and carried him down to Ballygall Road West – opposite the girl's school – to where the Blue Cross van was parked. There were other kids there with kittens and puppies and so on. There were some rabbits, as I recall. But no one else had a bird. Mum had given me 50 pence to put in the Blue Cross collection box. Everyone gave a small donation in return for the Vet's attention and treatment. I held my 50p in my hot little fist, anxiously waiting.

Then it was our turn. With Baby Pigeon tucked safely under my arm,

I hopped up into the van. Inside it was a bit like the mobile library. The Vet – towering over me – took Baby Pigeon out of the shoe box. Now, for a start, I didn't much like the casual way he held him. He was a little bit too casual. Not quite rough, but a bit too brisk. He held him briefly in his palm, took in the extended legs and asked me to open the pedal bin behind me.

Before I had time to take in the meaning of his words, he had wrung Baby Pigeon's little neck and in one fluid movement tossed him into the bin. Speechless with rage – this was no miracle vet – I fumbled with the pedal bin and reached in to get Baby Pigeon. But he had fallen down into the bottom and I simply couldn't reach him. As big, warm, wet tears fell and spattered on the floor, the nurse reached in past me and lifted him gently out. 'Now now,' she said. 'Here he is.'

'He's not for the bin,' I blurted as I put his broken body into my shoe box. As I ran for the door, the Vet called out something about a donation. As I exited, I managed to shout back at him – 'You'll never be in the *Readers Digest* – you fucking butcher!' Or words to that effect. Filled with moral outrage, I went home and buried Baby Pigeon in the rockery. Mum was sympathetic and we put the 50p into my Post Office savings account. My father told me that the vet was in all likelihood a 'ferocious gobshite'. There was some comfort in that.

The following year, in 1979, I left the dubious charms of primary school behind me. Traded Ballygall Road West for Ballygall Road East. Traded the rough company of Tommy Quinn and the other boys in my class for the tender mercies of the Christian Brothers.

In fact, as it happened, the Brothers in St Kevin's weren't so bad. There was some casual violence from time to time. Some gratuitous use of the leather. And one of the Brothers had a weapon he had brought home from Africa which consisted of a hickory ball attached to the end of an elephant's tendon. That's what he told us, in sadistic detail. He roamed the corridors liberally whalloping anyone in his path with it. But, it was done in a sort of good-humoured, robust, almost pally manner. If that makes any sense in the twenty-first century.

I enjoyed my time in St Kevin's. We had good teachers. Like all adolescents, we had good days and bad days. Despite the bad days there was endless encouragement in the school. Brother O'Connor – the principal – would urge us from time to time to 'be all that you can be'. A Kerryman, he watched me come and go over the five years. He would watch me acting the eejit at the gate, by the bike stand, or over by the bins. He never gave out to me. He would occasionally however ask me if I would realise my fullest potential. That sent a shiver up my spine. He even shouted it in exactly the same way my father did.

In sixth year, we had all of our religion classes rolled into one morning. The Brothers invited guest speakers to come and talk to us every Friday morning about life, the universe, everything. They ranged from local politicians, such as Prionsias de Rossa of the Worker's Party, to Fr Michael Cleary – the 'Working Man's Priest'.

Fr Cleary gave us a talk on contraception. Ironically. He likened the withdrawal method to 'trying to jump off the Dublin to Belfast train just as it got up to full speed around Swords'. We didn't really understand that. Neither did he, it would appear.

Six months later, after completing the Leaving Certificate in 1984, I was called to interview for Primary School Teacher Training. I was interviewed in Irish for a place in Colaiste Mhuire, Marino – the all-Irish teacher training college of Trinity College, Dublin. Part of the interview process required you to play a tune on a musical instrument. I was ready. I had resurrected my 48 bass accordion from the attic and had remastered 'Three Blind Mice'. As I queued for the music test, a collection of girls from all over Ireland, from Cork to Donegal, were practicing concert flutes, violins and other instruments in the hallway. It sounded like the warm up of the London philharmonic orchestra. I knew I was in trouble. A girl with uileann pipes was called. I was next. Through the door, I could hear her perform something akin to Riverdance. She might even have been dancing as well. I broke into a cold sweat as I heard her sing the scales and belt out two more traditional Irish folk songs. She sang them *sean nós*, or in the traditional, lilting 'old style'.

My turn. The examiner called me in and enquired in Irish what I intended to play. 'Three Blind Mice', I answered. He looked at me in astonishment. His astonishment grew as I arranged the sheet music before me on his desk. 'Em, I need the music to play it.' He folded his arms and sat back in his seat, gobsmacked. I played the tune. Badly – as I was nervous. It definitely wasn't my signature 'Three Blind Mice' that morning – the one that had saved me from a beating at the hands of Tommy Quinn.

'Can you sing something now?' he asked. 'Preferably, something in Irish.' Taking a deep breath, I started into the national anthem. He watched me sing it from start to finish. Watched me change key a few times. Watched me strangle the Soldier's Song. 'Well,' he said. 'I've never seen anything like that before.' I noticed that the corridor outside had also fallen silent. 'At least you can read music though,' he said.

As I walked through the corridor, around a hundred of Ireland's finest traditional musicians and *sean nós* singers – the pride of every convent school of Leaving Cert 1984 – stared at me with some incredulity. A month later, I was accepted into Primary School Teaching. I was later told that the Christian Brothers had written a very strong reference for me. Thank you Brother O'Connor, wherever you are.

# Chapter 7

# Teacher to Soldier

*All you need is a nice young man. And the army will do the rest.*

I graduated from Trinity College three years later. The teaching degree at Trinity was almost entirely through Irish. By graduation, I was certainly fluent in Irish writing. But, in terms of the spoken language, I could just about hold my own with the native Irish-speakers in my class. They were a forgiving group of peers who overlooked the manner in which I murdered the syntax, grammar and pronunciation of the language. It was a steep learning curve for a boy from Finglas. But I loved every minute of it. I particularly loved the liberal environment in Trinity and the fostering of critical enquiry. As a direct consequence, critical reflection was embedded within me and became an instinctive component of my emerging adult self. But, most of all, I loved the warmth of college life, the friendships, the debates and arguments, the collegial atmosphere and particularly the level of absolute acceptance among my peers.

An unexpected advantage of the course was the opportunity to study art. For the first time in my life, I received a formal training in it. I even got the opportunity to paint. I enjoyed the practical side of college too. Teaching practice, however, could be challenging. Especially so in some

Dublin schools, where the pupils regarded student teachers in much the same way as a pack of feral wolves might regard a tethered – however highly educated – sacrificial goat. My last teaching practice was with Sixth Class in St David's National School in Artane – a northside suburb of Dublin. I cycled there from Finglas each morning. On my first day, I got soaked in driving rain. Drenched from head to toe.

The teacher was sympathetic. He eyed his charges carefully and fixed on the tallest boy in the class. This surly eleven-year-old was ordered to 'Give Mr Clonan the tracksuit out of your gear bag.' I duly put it on. A Department of Education Inspector would never come on the first day of teaching practice – surely not?

An hour later, the Department of Education Inspector arrived. I was teaching PE to the class. They were in their tracksuits. I was in 'mine'. The Cigire stared at me with some interest. He took in the St David's Boys School tracksuit – which was admittedly a little tight on me. Eventually he pronounced his satisfaction and declared that I had taken a 'novel' and 'enthusiastic' approach to teaching PE and would probably act as a 'positive role model' for your average twelve-year-old.

That summer, I began applying for jobs. The summer of 1987 saw Ireland in deep recession. But I was one of the lucky ones and I managed to get work.

My first introduction to Scoil Mhuire National School in Lucan took place during that balmy summer. At the tender age of twenty, I was interviewed by the Principal, Henry Thynne and the Board of Management for the position of Sixth Assistant Teacher in the school. I remember being asked at the interview by the parish priest exactly how I would 'bring Jesus into the classroom'. My well-practised reply went something along the lines of, 'Father, my work as a teacher is a prayer which will bring Jesus directly into the hearts and minds of the boys and girls of

Scoil Mhuire.' I thought Henry looked a little bit sceptical, but the Padre was delighted. I got the job.

Teaching in Scoil Mhuire was certainly one of the most fulfilling experiences of my professional life. It was a great privilege to teach the children of Airlie and Woodview Heights in Lucan and I think I learned more from them and their parents than they ever learned from me.

I was very enthusiastic. I was also very young and inexperienced. My first car, a fifteen-year-old battered yellow Renault 12, would only start with a push. Every morning I parked it at the top of the slope in the staff car park. When school ended, I would get a selection of the bigger children to push-start me down the hill, where, engine screaming, I would rev the car into life just outside Henry's office window. I'd blow the horn and the kids would give a wild cheer. They seemed to enjoy this great adventure. Back then, I had yet to hear of the phrase 'health and safety'. After about a week of these antics, Henry called me aside and asked me if it would not be simpler to go out and buy a battery for the car. I got the hint and thus ended the daily mayhem in the staff car park.

Henry proved to be a great mentor, colleague and friend. He coached me constantly and advised me to think about the future. And I had been thinking about the future. During my first year of teaching, I drove with friends to Achill Island on the west coast for the St Patrick's Day weekend. It was an idyllic weekend on the Atlantic coast. The sun shone. The Guinness flowed. And then, on 19 March 1988, at a traditional Irish music session in a pub on Achill, the owner rushed into the bar and called for silence. He looked distressed. The entire pub fell into silence as he fumbled with the remote control of the television behind the bar. We then saw the live TV images of two British Army corporals being beaten and shot to death in west Belfast. The tourists were speechless. It was a low point.

The Troubles had always constituted a strong back-beat to my childhood and adolescence. The 1980s were a dark decade in Ireland. In economic terms, we were a basket case. Charles Haughey had told us we were living beyond our means and that we needed to tighten our belts. In parallel with this, the dual campaigns of violence – those waged by both the Provisional IRA and the British Army and their loyalist proxies – were reaching a crescendo. Both the IRA and the British establishment seemed locked in a struggle that would ultimately have led – were it not for the peace process – to an outcome of Balkan proportions. The IRA had almost managed to wipe out Margaret Thatcher's cabinet in the Brighton Bombing of 1984. In 1988 and 1989, new levels of savagery were being reached in the conflict in Ireland and in Britain. On the one hand, the indiscriminate bombing and shooting of innocent civilians by terrorists. And on the other, a deliberate shoot-to-kill policy waged by the British security forces. As Europe was moving forward – with the collapse of Communism and the Berlin Wall – Ireland was going backwards.

In this environment of economic austerity, mass emigration and violence, I found myself, day after day, teaching the children in my care about an idea of Ireland, an idealised notion of Irish society, that simply did not exist. I found myself as a young adult, as a young teacher, more and more troubled by the economic and political challenges we were facing outside of the classroom. I found myself more and more vocal in my criticism of both the Provisional IRA on the one hand and the British security forces on the other. They seemed locked in a mutually reinforcing cycle of violence that was eroding Ireland's political, economic and social cohesion.

Ireland in the 1980s was Ireland on hold. And as a teacher – purporting to teach young citizens about an Ireland that was indefinitely postponed through violence and economic stagnation – I felt I was a young man on hold. I decided then – foolishly, naively or otherwise – that I needed to make a different kind of contribution to Irish society. And, naive and idealistic as I was, I decided to join the Army. My naive belief at the time was that if service in the military could save even one life, or contribute in even the smallest way to a more peaceful, prosperous Ireland – where freedom of speech was possible without having to look over one's shoulder – then it would be worth it. I also wanted to break out of the confinement of the classroom and the nine-to-five routine. I wanted – as the Irish Army now puts it – a 'life less ordinary'. And I certainly got that. In spades.

So, after two years of teaching in Scoil Mhuire, I was finally accepted as an officer cadet in the Irish army. Maybe I would have been better off studying law or getting involved in politics. But I was an idealistic young man, with what my Dad had described as a 'heightened sense of justice'. Probably the worst reason in the world to join any army. Anywhere.

So, in November 1989, I received my joining instructions for the 66th Cadet Class. I said goodbye to Henry and my class of eight-year-olds in Lucan. My parents drove me to the Curragh Camp on 6 November 1989 – a date which is seared into my memory. It was here that I got my first taste of the Curragh Camp. Located in County Kildare, approximately thirty miles south west of Dublin's city centre, it is the only purpose-built garrison town in Ireland – a vast complex of nineteenth-century redbrick buildings abandoned by the British during the War of Independence. It is a place where time has stood still for the best part of a century. A Victorian town frozen in time and place. A peculiar visual reminder of the British Army's occupation of Ireland. It is also miserably cold.

As an idealistic and relatively naive young man, nothing could have prepared me for my introduction to life as an officer in the Irish army. The Cadet School itself – physically resembling a forbidding and gloomy Hogwarts – was housed in Pearse Barracks. It was in Pearse Barracks that I began my army career as a shaven headed army cadet. The lowest of the low in the hierarchy of the Irish armed forces.

I had given up all of my newly acquired adult freedoms to train as a cadet. I exchanged autonomy for eighteen months of virtual detention and intense military training within the confines of the Cadet School. The experience was an enormous culture shock for me. The training at times felt like imprisonment with hard labour. For me and my fellow cadets, there would be no remission; all eighteen months of intensive training were to be served consecutively. With no time off for good behaviour. Physically and psychologically, it was the most challenging experience of my life up to that point.

The training regime was extremely tough. Intensive weapons training and tactics at first. Then military history, military law, military administration, politics, economics and leadership. We learned everything the hard way. The training was certainly thorough, if a little anachronistic at times. For, in much the same way that the Irish Army had inherited most of its physical infrastructure from the British Army of the 1920s – its ancient garrisons, regulations and even weapons – so also had it inherited much of the cultural infrastructure of the British Army of that era. Hence, within the Cadet School there was an unforgiving and unapologetic emphasis on brutal physical training known as 'endurance training' or more ominously 'combat training'. There was also an emphasis on negative reinforcement and punishment within the Cadet School – through its standard operating procedures, regulations and standing orders.

The motivation to compete and fight was built into every aspect of life in the Cadet School. And it was in this competitive and combative environment that I was selected to represent the Cadet School in the *Irish Times* Debating Competition. The debating style was no-holds-barred. I first debated against my old alma mater, Trinity. I then debated in UCD, UCC and in the Kings Inns. A series of raucous affairs with a lot of heckling and so on. But, as a Cadet, failure was not an option, and I managed to win every debate, hands down. I think I was driven by fear of failure and the desire to get a respite from the privations of Pearse Barracks. I eventually got to the final and won as individual speaker. This resulted in a debating tour of the United States – and a one-month escape from the Cadet School. I recall my commanding officer congratulating me at the time – complimenting me on my competitive and persistent debating style, 'Like a Jack Russell snapping at a bag of sausages.'

The US tour was a high point for me. I spent some time in the US Air Force Academy in Colorado Springs while I was there and got a taste of American military culture. Cadets are the same everywhere was my conclusion. Especially when it came to drinking and hell raising whilst negotiating the rigours of military life. As one Air Force Cadet put it to me, 'The military is all about three things. Kicking ass, kissing ass and chasing ass.' For me, it was definitely about getting my ass kicked most of the time.

Then, a return to the Curragh and the relentless continuation of training. Days beginning with check parade at 6 AM. On live exercises or 'on the ground' as we referred to such manoeuvres, we would be placed under severe mental and physical pressure for days and nights on end with little sleep – and no sympathy. We were groomed remorselessly and endlessly for command by our training officers and NCOs. The Non Commissioned Officers – the sergeants and corporals who conducted much of the nuts and bolts of our training – were the best in the Irish

Army. To us they were terrifying. They drove us to the outer limits of our endurance. As did our training officers. I remember one of our officers telling me in a matter-of-fact way that in order to train someone to kill, 'All you need is a nice young man. And the army will do the rest.'

And the Army did the rest. When we were finally commissioned as young officers, we had been so effectively trained in the management and use of force that it had become second nature to all of us. Each and every one of us was intimately acquainted with the legal and operational conditions within which it was considered legitimate to seriously wound or kill others. Something we were trained to assess on a split-second basis. The question 'Would you kill someone?' became something of an in-house joke. It wasn't a matter of ethics, or moral hesitation. Just a quick mental assessment to see if the killing would 'meet the legal criteria'.

In this way, the Cadet School produced excellent officers for the combat arms. The experience brought about a dramatic transformation in each of us. The Irish army taught us about fighting as the underdog. It taught to exploit to the maximum whatever minimal assets one could mobilise in the most pressurized situation – against whatever odds. Never, ever, ever give up. A philosophy no doubt inherited from the Army's guerrilla origins. Most of all, the Irish Army demanded at all times the maximum exploitation of one's self.

Failure was not an option for any cadet. And many of the 66th Cadet Class did fail. Those that failed were discharged. Those of us that survived the Darwinian process learned to respect our training officers in that they had also come through the same system. And when commissioned, we went, almost overnight, from being 'the lowest of the low' within the army to being welcomed – with open arms – into the heart of the officer corps. The day I was commissioned as an officer in the Irish Army was the proudest day of my life. It was the only time I had seen my father shed even the briefest of tears. He told me that there was 'a breeze [in the Curragh] that would take the eye out of your head.'

My mother told me she thought the camp was 'lovely'. 'You must have had a lovely time my love,' she said. She took in my classmates. Temporarily insane after eighteen months of captivity and organised mayhem. 'They look like lovely boys.'

By making it through the Cadet School, we had automatically earned the respect of our fellow officers. Learning to earn the respect of one's NCOs and subordinates was an entirely different matter. That would take years.

For me, that process would begin not far from the Curragh Camp. Having finished in the top ten of the 66th Cadet Class, I got my first choice of appointment and was posted as a newly commissioned officer to an artillery unit – the Third Battery, based in Magee Barracks, Kildare Town. I made myself busy. In the first year or so, I completed all of the artillery courses necessary to become an instructor in the School of Artillery in the Combat Support College. During that time, I also completed a Masters degree in communications in Dublin City University. I was selected to take over the military training of the 37th Apprentice Platoon in the Army's Apprentice School in Naas. I was subsequently selected to train a recruit platoon of gunners in Kildare. Time passed quickly for me. Adjusting to the day-to-day garrison routine of the Irish Army. The learning curve was steep. But it was about to get a lot steeper. For within four years of my date of commission, I was to find myself in command of troops in what the military refers to euphemistically as a 'live operational environment' in the Middle East.

Al Yatun would prove an education in itself, unlike any other I had experienced before. Or since.

# Chapter 8

# The Compounds

*Wednesday, 18 October 1995*

And, so that's how I got here. Now I'm awake on the floor of a filthy billet somewhere in South Lebanon. Now I remember. After dreaming of scorpions all night, I shake myself out of the sleeping bag and hit the shower block. It is 5.30 AM and Al Yatun is wide awake. There is a queue for the showers. Troops using parka jackets as dressing gowns in the morning chill.

As I'm shaving, a commotion starts in the shower area. There is uproar among the Dubs. 'Watch out will ya, there's a fuckin snake in the head.' And sure enough, a large black snake coils out of one of the toilet cubicles and slithers across the tiles. It is about five feet long, jet black and its tongue is flickering – just like the snakes I've seen in *National Geographic*. 'What'll we do Sir?' shouts one of the lads.

'Ehh,' I reply.

Corporal Burke has unrolled his towel and is attempting to shoo the snake out the door. I hear his Donegal accent clearly. 'Go on ye wee black bastard, I'm only tryin to have a shower now.' The snake has now risen on its coils and is swaying menacingly to and fro amongst the throng. Half the guys are buck naked. The rest have only the protection of flip flops and towels. Pandemonium has broken loose.

Suddenly, the snake flexes itself and like a whip snaps across the floor and exits under the door. It then loops under the steps and disappears under the shower block, which is raised about three feet above ground level. The entire shower block is perched on top of four sets of cavity blocks at each corner. Some of the lads have followed the snake out the door and are peering into the gloom under the shower block. My heart rate is beginning to return to normal.

Another cheer erupts from outside. Two of the lads have crawled in after the snake. One has a Swiss Army Knife – with the ridiculously small blade open at one end and the cork screw opened at the other. 'Go on Johnny – kill that fuckin snake!' 'Cut off his bleedin' head!' There is a rumpus under the floorboards and I can hear Johnny's muffled shouts. 'C'mere ye fucker ye.' I've had enough and head for my grimy billet to get into uniform.

There is a roar of approval from behind me. Johnny, it seems, has emerged with the wriggling snake. He has been bitten several times and has a desperate hold of the writhing creature. A Company's CS appears on the scene.

'PUT THAT FUCKIN' SERPENT DOWN! IT COULD BE A FUCKIN' POISONOUS ONE!'

Johnny protests. 'It could be our mascot.'

The CS addresses the group in the shower block, 'We already have mascots over in the officers mess.' There is much laughter. The CS then notices me among the group. 'Beggin' your pardon Sir – didn't recognise you in your towel.' There is more laughter. The snake disappears into a stone gabion. I slam the door of my billet behind me. I'm convinced that I am surrounded by maniacs.

Later on, I'm up on the roof of the officer's mess with the commanding officer of A Company. Commandant McManus is giving the junior officers a visual orientation of the AO. That's when I see them first. Directly opposite us, less than 2km away, on the ridgeline, bathed in the early morning sunshine, are the Israeli hilltop firebases. There are around a dozen in all – stretching from Bayt Lif south of us overlooking the villages of Rshaf, across to Bayt Yahun, Brashit and north up to Shaqrah, Houle and Markabe. All of the high points overlooking the AO are dominated by the IDF and SLA firebases. Each is designated by the prefix Delta Foxtrot Foxtrot – DFF – followed by a numbered serial. From the roof of Al Yatun, I note the positions of DFF 12, DFF 13, DFF 17 and so on – up to DFF 30 and DFF 109 to the north east.

The hilltop firebases are massive, fortified positions bristling with weapons, antennae and anti-missile defences. They are inherently unnatural – black, asymmetrical structures. Their angular, sinister profiles are at odds with the otherwise uninterrupted topography of the opposing ridgeline. From our observation posts, we occasionally see movement. Usually a weapon system traversing or a range finder locking on to some distant target. Rarely do we see human activity. The firebases are otherworldly. They are in sharp contrast to our brightly painted white UN positions. Our positions are brightly illuminated, night and day. At night, the Israeli positions remain in darkness.

On this bright morning in October, the firebases are silent. Commandant McManus lists the weapons systems contained within each base. A mix of direct and indirect fire weapons. Heavy machine guns, missile systems, mortars. Some have tanks dug into the earthen banks to provide High Explosive Anti-Tank (HEAT) and High Explosive Anti-Personnel (HEAP) direct fire capability. All have interlocking arcs of fire to provide 360-degree protection from Hizbullah attack. Commandant McManus finishes his inventory by asking us to consider the determination of the Hizbullah fighters who regularly assault the posts on foot. Hizbullah have been attacking the hilltop positions for years. Their attacks are no longer suicide missions. Hizbullah are becoming more sophisticated, with coordinated attacks on the Israeli compounds. The consequent increase in IDF and SLA casualties has provoked a brutal response from the firebases. They are jumpy. When they perceive a threat, they open up with everything they've got – in a full 360-degree arc of fire. This is referred to euphemistically as 'reconnaissance by fire'. It is unforgiving. If you are caught in the open when the IDF opens fire – you will become a casualty. 'Watch yourselves out there. Those weapons systems don't discriminate between Hizbullah, Irishbatt personnel, civilians or goats for that matter.' It is a sobering brief.

We then begin our ground orientation. Lieutenant Murphy walks me to our fleet of APCs. I'm lost in my own thoughts. I'm beginning to reflect a little more critically on the dubious glamour of being in the Battalion's '911 service'. Maybe my Dad was right after all. Maybe there was some other 'fucking eejit' who'd do this job. I am beginning to feel distinctly uneasy.

The BMR is split into two Mobile Support Groups or MSGs. Each MSG consists of three vehicles. An AML 90 armoured fighting vehicle – usually at the front – followed by two APCs. Our mission is to constantly patrol the Irish AO and to act as its rapid response unit to any incident, day or night – 24/7, the BMR is tasked with intervention, reinforcement and proactive engagement in any scenario.

The BMR's APCs are Finnish-manufactured Sisu vehicles. These massive six-wheeled vehicles are equipped with 10mm of armour. Not a lot of protection, but they are huge – they can carry up to sixteen fully armed troops – and they are fast. They have a top speed of over 100km per hour – despite being over 13 tonnes in weight. The Irish APCs are painted white with bold UN lettering. Blue UN flags are attached prominently. At night they are lit up with small searchlights bolted on to the armour plate. The idea is that we are immediately and unmistakably identifiable as UN – to all parties in the conflict. Sergeant Bracken remarks drily that this makes it all the easier to target us – 'by all parties to the conflict.' Particularly at night.

Each APC is armed with twin general purpose machine guns in the weapons turret. We carry over 4,000 rounds of ammunition for these. Belts of armour piercing, tracer and high velocity 7.62 bullets are checked before each patrol. Each APC also carries an 84mm recoilless anti-tank weapon. We carry nine missiles for each 84mm – three High Explosive Anti-Tank, three High Explosive Anti-Personnel and three Illumination rounds. In addition, each member of the BMR carries their own Steyr automatic assault rifle and ammunition.

The vehicles are equipped with large radios known as '46 sets' to monitor the battalion net. Smaller '77 Sets' monitor the individual Company radio net – depending on which sector of Irishbatt's AO we are operating in. We also have an internal radio net so that the officer in command can communicate with the crew – driver, observer and gunner. The officer also carries a handheld Motorola radio for direct communications with Battalion Headquarters and the Operations Officer. The result is a lot – an awful lot – of radio chatter. As a junior officer it is no easy task to follow the thread of four separate radio conversations whilst reading a map, and remaining in control. The task of patrol commander is not for the faint hearted. And that's before the shit hits the fan.

The Sisu APCs are accompanied on patrol by AML 90 armoured fighting vehicles. The firepower in the large APCs is augmented by these nimble 4x4 armoured vehicles. Equipped with a 90mm main armament, they are capable of taking out most vehicles – or obstacles to escape – at short range. Each AML 90 carries twenty 90mm rounds of HEAT and HEAP for the main gun. In addition, the AML 90s also have coaxial mounted twin general purpose machine guns. Each carries 2,000 rounds of 7.62 mixed ammunition on patrol.

As we roll out the gate and the radios whir into life – I realise that the BMR's mission will place us at the heart of any action taking place in our 100 square kilometre patch. I also realise that this is the reason we are carrying so much ammunition. For the first time in my army career, I feel the weight of responsibility. The weight of command on my shoulders. Because when we roll out the gate, It'll be me in charge. No one to turn to for a second opinion. Lieutenant Murphy – who has squeezed up beside me in the rear observation hatch – is taking particular delight in reminding me of my various responsibilities. 'Your map is upside-down Tommy,' is his first observation. There may be trouble ahead indeed.

Lieutenant Murphy directs our first patrol on a wide sweep of the Irishbatt AO, through all the approved A, B and C Company routes and tracks. We refer to each company area as Alpha, Bravo and Charlie routes. We call in to each Company Headquarters and he introduces me to the various Irish operations staff in Haddathah and Brashit. They tell me of any activity in each Company area and what routes have been swept for mines, booby traps and unexploded ordnance. The familiarisation patrol takes hours. We are constantly drinking water to stay hydrated. A plume of dust marks our progress across rutted tracks and *bóithríní* (small lanes) of sticky tarmac. All the while, we are within sight – or range – of the Israeli firebases. No matter where you are in the Irishbatt AO – one is overlooked by an Israeli hilltop position.

All of the villages we pass through are bustling with activity. Donkeys, goats, cats, dogs, children, chickens – all manner of creatures and all age groups throng the narrow streets as we pass through. The newer buildings at the edge of the villages are all un-rendered, un-plastered concrete dwellings. In the village centres, the concrete gives way to dusty, dung-coloured buildings. Some are plastered. Some rendered with a rough wattle and daub mixture. All manner of commerce thrives in the villages. And in no predictable pattern. Hairdressers, grocery shops, butchers, mechanics, pharmacies vie alongside stalls of every description. Many of the villages are in a pitiable condition.

Everywhere, the bare concrete and plastered walls are pocked with bullet holes. Many rooftops – and most of the upper stories of buildings – have been raked with automatic gunfire of one sort or another. Many have been holed by tank shells. Some bear the marks of direct hits fired from Israeli helicopter gunships. Today, my first day, is quiet. The children run alongside the APCs, laughing and cat-calling in Arabic. Older people ignore us. The only adults who wave are the stall holders, shopkeepers and 'Mingy Men' who ply their trade under our minimal protection.

All along the roadside are posters bearing the grim faces of Hizbullah 'martyrs' who have died attacking the hilltop positions.

Chapter 9

# Mary Robinson Wears No Knickers

*I want this Presidency to promote the telling of stories – stories of celebration through the arts and stories of conscience and of social justice.*

Her Excellency Mary Robinson, President of Ireland and Commander in Chief of the Irish Defence Forces

Having exhausted all of the routes in Irishbatt – and having exhausted me in the process – Spud Murphy decides to direct our familiarisation patrol into the neighbouring Ghanaian Battalion area. I have never felt further from home in this alien environment. Like the Wild Geese and millions of Irish before me, I have to adjust to a new and strange country. So we proceed beyond Irishbatt towards Tyre. The Ghanaian Battalion – or Ghanbatt – Area of Operations lies just to the north of Irishbatt. As the BMR regularly passes through Ghanbatt on convoy escorts to the coastal cities of Tyre and Beirut, Spud reckons it is a good idea to continue our familiarisation patrol towards Deir Ntar. Apparently Deir Ntar also has very good coffee.

We pass through a major Ghanaian checkpoint. As we rumble through the chicane and bounce over the dusty speed ramps, the Ghanaians smile broadly at us. There is a very good relationship it seems between the Irish and the 'Ghans', as they are affectionately known by the Paddies. The checkpoint commander reaches up to high-five myself and Spud Murphy. He roars up at us, 'On the Big Irish Ball', whilst tracing a circular motion with his index finger. Spud shouts into his mouthpiece and I hear his crackly voice in my ears over the noise of the engines. 'Watch this, Tommy.'

Spud leans over the side of the APC and shouts, 'Azumah Nelson is a woman!' Azumah is one of Ghana's most famous sporting heroes – a boxer and role model for millions of Ghanaian men. The Ghanaian soldier freezes. He is rooted to the spot by Spud's declaration. I hear Spud cackling in my headset. The Ghanaian recovers quickly though and sprints to catch up with us before we exit the checkpoint. 'Mary Robinson wears no knickers!' he screeches in response. We laugh until we cry. Unfortunately however, 'Mary Robinson wears no knickers' becomes a universal greeting for the Irish that spreads among the other contingents. The Ghans have had the last laugh.

We have coffee in Deir Ntar. The first of many hundreds of bitter black coffees I will have in Lebanon. The beginning of an addiction. As we make our way back to Al Yatun, Spud points out the 'shops' that have sprung up around Irishbatt's positions. I use the term 'shops' loosely. Just outside Camp Shamrock there is a collection of ramshackle concrete lean-tos with corrugated iron roofs. Irish soldiers, weapons slung over their backs, are gathered around one called 'Saddam Burger'. It advertises 'Very Beautiful Burger'. There is also apparently a 'Dunnes Stores' in the vicinity of Total.

We pass by another collection of sheds bearing a huge sign which reads, somewhat dubiously, 'Ilac Centre'. The 'Mingy Shops' as they are known, supply the Irish troops with a bewildering array of goods and services. From laundry and ironing, to toothpaste, chocolate, 'Scud-Burgers'

– don't ask – to jewellery, exotic lingerie and a comprehensive and slightly frightening library of pornographic movies. They also sell 'pharmaceutical products' that are popular with the troops. These include 'Al Zobra – Penis Enlargment Pils [sic]' to 'Fat-Busters Pils [sic]'.

The 'Mingy Men' who run the shops are larger-than-life characters. Since Ireland's first deployment to the Lebanon in the 1970s, the Mingy Men have become intimately acquainted with the odd shopping habits of the Irish male. Over the decades, the Mingy Men have observed the quirky purchasing patterns of bored, cash-rich Irish soldiers who – sometimes fuelled by guilt, loneliness or drink, or all three – buy hundreds of thousands of dollars worth of crap in their shops each year. By and large, the Mingy Men will have the measure of most Irishmen within seconds of meeting them. I was to find that I was no exception in this regard.

The magnificently titled 'Ali Strawballs' is the proprietor of the Mingy shop outside B Company Headquarters in Haddathah. Rosie runs the shop outside C Company HQ in Brashit. I am told – by dozens of 'concerned' soldiers over the coming months – that 'unfortunately' Rosie does not sell porno movies.

In Al Yatun, we have Hafif. He has been nicknamed 'Hafif the Thief' by the Dubs in position 6-40. Hafif doesn't like this. On more than one occasion during my tour of duty he asks me to get the troops to call him, 'Hafif the Honest Man'. This proves impossible and provokes much loud and ribald speculation as to Hafif's moral and ethical orientation. Such speculation is rife – coming as it does from the brutal and licentious soldiery of A Company and the BMR – as to Hafif's sexual orientation and preferred methods of torture in the event of one's inability to pay one's bill or in the event of a Hizbullah invasion of our position. 'Hafif'd ride ye all the way to Tyre and back for a fiver.'

After our orientation patrol, we retire to the officer's mess for a debrief. The whitewashed villa also houses the operations cell and our communications centre. There is a machine gun post on the roof which overlooks the checkpoint at the entrance to the post. It is manned 24/7 by troops from A Company. Meanwhile, below, the communications centre is manned by Corporal 'Psycho' Dunne. He is completely bald, and bears a remarkable and unsettling resemblance to Nosferatu. Apparently, he never leaves the gloomy interior of the communications centre. Psycho also operates the public address system in Al Yatun. He does this in his own inimitable style. All messages are delivered deadpan in his distinctive flat Dublin accent. 'Attention all personnel – the so-called Muktar has arrived to meet and greet with the green, I mean, new, officers.'

Spud pushes me out the door. 'You have to meet the Muktar.' We cross to the vehicle park where a large black Mercedes is parked. A group of curious A Company troops have gathered to observe the formalities. The Muktar – Rafik Haydar Hazimi – emerges from the Merc. He is ancient and has about him a retinue of heavily bearded and rather aggressive looking men from the village. Spud motions me forward. I offer my hand to the Muktar. But he does not respond. Instead, he is staring at me open-mouthed. He looks to his entourage and speaks Arabic in a low, urgent voice. Then he addresses me.

'You are Captain Cloonan?' he asks incredulously.

'Err, Lieutenant Clonan,' I correct him.

His eyes narrow. 'But, Lieutenant Spud Murphy is big man. Very big man.' Spud nods in agreement. The Muktar continues. 'Lieutenant McCarthy was very big man. Lieutenant O'Connor was big man. And, Lieutenant O'Brien was very big man – with red hair.' As he lists what seems like every Irish officer posted to Al Yatun over the previous decade – the troops are pushing closer, enjoying the discussion immensely. One of the A Company privates is particularly helpful.

'Muktar – do ya remember Lieutenant Ryan, he was six foot six.'

The Muktar wheels around and points his bony finger in the air. 'Yes, Lieutenant Ryan was very big man.'

At this point the Muktar fixes his gaze on me once more. 'But, you – you are very small man.' 'Smallest Lieutenant in Al Yatun – ever,' he adds for emphasis. There is silence. The troops watch me expectantly. Then the Muktar seems to relent. Perhaps he feels that he has committed some social faux pas. He approaches me – and in a scene straight out of Laurence of Arabia – grabs me in a sudden embrace. He kisses me on both cheeks and grabs my wrist. Gripping my hand triumphantly over-head – he shouts to all those assembled. 'Lieutenant Clonan is small man. Yes. This is the will of Allah. But. I tell you truthfully. He is very beauti-ful.' There is an enthusiastic round of applause from the troops accompa-nied by loud whistles. Pleased with himself, the Muktar then joins us for coffee.

For months afterwards, every time I roll out the gates of Al Yatun on patrol, the comedians on the checkpoint shout up at me, 'Are ye off to the Muktar's house for coffee?' BS Begley interrupts on the headset. 'Ignore them emptyheads, Sir. Forgive them. For they know not what they do.'

That evening we have dinner in the mess. A local boy Khalid Hakim acts as our waiter and general factotum. We each make a contribution towards his wages. Khalid is saving his dollars to go to the Technical University in Beirut where he hopes to become a mobile telephone engineer. We eat the same rations as the troops – our meals come directly from the cookhouse. However, we also contribute to a cash pool for bottles of Chateau Kafraya or Chateau Musar – Lebanese wines. The Lebanese wine is excellent. It will also help to take the edge off the all-male, brutal environment that is Al Yatun.

Khalid announces the evening's menu. 'Chicken in a flak jacket' is breaded chicken. 'Chicken with thing' is stuffed chicken. 'Not chicken' is any other meat. 'Red thing' is carrots. 'Green thing' is any other vegetable. 'Spuds' is potatoes. 'White thing' is pasta or rice. Tonight, Khalid announces, 'Not Chicken, Red thing, White thing and Cook Corporal says dessert is that fucking rice thing.' There goes our Michelin Star.

As darkness descends on Al Yatun, those troops that are not on checkpoints, observation posts or patrols retire to the pre-fabs and their bunks. Many write letters. Others read. All are lonely.

# Chapter 10

# Bodies in the Wadis

*78 Irishbatt Operations Summary October 1995 – After a period of calm, Israeli Defence Forces fire on Irish positions at the end of October – Logged as 'Firings Close to Irishbatt Positions'*
*Serials One (1) – Nine (9) – 05.05Hrs – 21.37 Hrs*

Unit History, 78 Irishbatt, UNIFIL

The night time routine in Al Yatun is repetitive and confined. Some head out to Hafif's shop at the entrance to the post. Hafif has arranged plastic garden furniture under a crude wooden veranda outside the shop. Soldiers sit, rifles slung casually over their shoulders or across their knees drinking coffee or chai. Hafif has installed a clay oven in the rear of the shop in which he is baking 'Double Doubles'. This is a culinary speciality that Hafif has custom designed for the Dublin troops of Al Yatun. A 'Double Double' consists of a hefty portion of greasy chips, with grilled 'chicken' wrapped up in a double layer of locally produced flat breads. This sticky mess is liberally smothered in a yellow creamy goo which Hafif calls mayonnaise. The chicken is also of indeterminate origin. One of the seasoned veterans claims that he has seen Hafif's cousin shooting seagulls at one of the tip-heads in Tibnine.

It is true that the locals love to shoot birds. All types. From crows to songbirds of all sizes – no matter how small. It is not unusual to see local men and boys wandering through the checkpoint with small calibre rifles and dozens of small birds hanging from their belts. They are all eaten and the smaller birds are considered a particular delicacy. Under the UN Security Council Resolution for Lebanon, the locals are permitted to carry small calibre weapons for hunting and pest control. The locals refer to this as the 'Shoot the Bird' law. Otherwise, for all other weapons of larger calibres, we are required to disarm all armed elements at our checkpoints – by force if necessary. This leads to frequent armed stand-offs between Irish soldiers and Hizbullah or other Islamic resistance groups who refuse to hand over AK-47s and other weapons. We call these 'Mexican stand-offs'. When they happen, the BMR is called out to intervene.

As for me, the routine for the next seven months will follow an endlessly recurring three-day cycle. On day one, I am patrol officer for the BMR. That means I am the patrol commander of the day. During that twenty-four-hour period I will mount six separate armoured patrols during the period 6 AM to 6 AM the following morning. At least two of the patrols must be between midnight and 6 AM. The timings of the patrols are varied by the Operations Officer at Battalion Headquarters. He or she also decides the routes to be followed for each patrol. The patrol routine is varied to avoid roadside bomb attacks, ambushes or landmines. We patrol through A, B and C Company areas which we term Alpha, Bravo and Charlie routes. In addition to these patrols, we are liable to attend any incident that occurs throughout the Irish Battalion AO as they arise. We are also on-call for incidents in the neighbouring battalion areas.

Day two consists of a mandatory sleep period from 6 AM to midday. I am then tasked as Duty Officer for the BMR until 6 AM of day three.

Day three is 'standby' day. On this day I am required to command reinforcements should more than one incident occur at any point within the AO. On day three I am also expected to deal with all other tasks associated with command including man management, discipline, logistics, administration and training. We are expected to maintain our own physical fitness in addition to our other tasks. During the deployment we will be required to pass at least two exacting fitness tests.

And so the days begin to accelerate and blur into a continuous loop of day patrols and patrols in darkness. The daytime patrols are exceptionally hot. Daytime temperatures in October rise to over 30 degrees centigrade, made hotter by the constant heat and vibration from the massive diesel engines in the Sisus. And hotter again wearing helmet, flak jacket and carrying weapons and ammunition. Each time the vehicle stops, we dismount and walk some of the route, familiarising ourselves with the villages and water holes, the wadis and the ridgelines. All the while overlooked by the Israeli firebases, their weapons tracking us slowly as we traverse our patrol routes.

Occasionally we see Hizbullah, driving at breakneck speed in old beat-up Mercedes – with telltale radio sets perched on dashboards. Aerials at low angles out windows. We drink litre upon litre of water to stay hydrated. The water is warm but we don't care. We drink continuously. If you don't, you get sleepy, lethargic, unable to think straight. The days pass quickly for Irishbatt. The incoming troops become gradually tanned. The outgoing battalion disappear over the three rotation days of October. By Halloween, they are all at home in Ireland. Even Spud is gone. We assume full operational command of Irishbatt. I'm on my own.

I am also lulled into a false sense of security. Nothing of note has happened in October. Although we are exhausted most of the time, we are becoming accustomed to the routine. Familiar with the road and track networks. No longer relying on the map for orientation. Commandant

McManus however constantly reminds us of the febrile nature of south Lebanon. The relative quiet is deceptive. Fickle. We know that Hizbullah are increasingly active in our area. We see more and more young men from Tyre and Sidon driving through the villages. Especially at night. They are angry young men who glower at us as we pass them on patrol. They glare at us as we mentally take note of their vehicle details, plate numbers and descriptions for our reports to Battalion Headquarters. I count them. I note their clothing. Sweatshirts, jeans, trainers. American logos and designer tags seem out of place in this environment.

And then it happens. At 5.05 AM on Tuesday, 31 October, Hizbullah launch a dawn attack on five of the Israeli hilltop positions. They mount coordinated attacks on DFF 13, known as the Cuckoo's Nest, and DFF 17, known as Haddathah Compound, in the Irishbatt AO. These Israeli firebases are directly south of Al Yatun. I am in the communications centre when it happens. Psycho is talking to me when suddenly I can no longer hear his voice. A deafening roar drowns out his words. It happens so quickly that my brain is not processing the noise. And then vibration. My body takes over though and I drop to the floor in a moment of reflex. Like when I was a small boy playing cowboys and Indians. Taking cover. Only I didn't do it consciously. The noise is so great, the vibration so violent that I've done this involuntarily. Adrenaline rushing through me. Pins and needles in my fingers. I look up at Psycho. He is leaning over the desk looking at me with concern. 'That's Katyushas Sir – outgoin. Relax will ya? Yer makin me nervous.'

The radios crank into life. I am beginning to make sense of what's happening when a dawn chorus of new sounds commences. The cacophony of radio chatter is drowned out by a series of loud thuds. The floor is shaking. As though a giant was stamping his feet around the building. Now Psycho is crouched low. A split second later we hear the deafening explosions. Incoming fire. The Israelis are now saturating the area with defensive artillery fire. What is known as 'suppressing fire'. The radio, slower than the speed of sound, slower than the speed of incoming rounds, announces, 'Gate 12 has opened fire.'

'We fuckin' know that,' says Psycho.

Then the Israeli firebases open up. There is the insistent thump, thump, thump of heavy machine guns – or 'point fives' as we call them. Overlaying that is a curious thudding noise. Like a large sledgehammer beating the earth. 'Fuckin' mortars,' observes Psycho. Then there is the furious chatter of machine gun fire. High velocity rounds slapping and whining in all directions from the compounds directly opposite us. Then the screeching of incoming artillery once more. 'That's fuckin' rate 6,' shouts Psycho. In other words, the Israeli artillery battery at Gate 12 beyond Al Mafqa are firing six rounds of High Explosive Anti-Personnel per minute. One artillery salvo every ten seconds. Psycho crawls over to the PA system and announces, 'Attention all personnel, Groundhog, Groundhog, Groundhog – If you didn't already know it – Flak jackets and helmets – Report to the bunkers. All BMR and DUTY personnel report to the communications centre.'

The officers of A Company arrive one by one into the communications centre. We are grinning nervously at each other – especially the new guys. Commandant McManus looks at me. 'Why are you still here?' he asks. 'You'd want to shake your guys out and prep your vehicles.' That's when it dawns on me that I don't really want to go outside. Into all that noise and mayhem. It's, well, dangerous.

I suppress those thoughts and force myself to sprint off in the direction of the vehicle park. Like running underwater. Out into the noise. The rear doors of the SISU are slightly open. BS Begley reaches down and hauls me into the rear of the vehicle. 'I've the kettle on,' he says.

Everyone is smirking. Gunner Molloy is checking the ammunition for the anti-tank weapon. Trooper Kavanagh is placing ammunition belts on to the gun turret. I wonder what my Mum and Dad are doing now. Probably asleep at home in Ballygall Avenue. Unaware. Oblivious. I think about all my school friends. My classmates in college. Fuck this. I could be wandering home from Copperface Jack's just now. Not looking around the APC at a group of individuals who are obviously half mad. The vehicle shakes and shudders as the artillery rounds impact around us. 'Milk?' asks BS Begley.

'Eh, yeah, no sugar though.'

The radios are alive with traffic. 'Hello Zero – Firing close at 640. I say again, firing close. Origin Uniform Kilo.' Uniform Kilo is the phonetic code for UK or unknown. There is so much shit being fired at us at this point that no one can keep track of who is firing what at whom. All the while, the Operations Cell in Irishbatt HQ keep up a steady monotone on the radio. 'Roger your last. Account for all personnel. Log and record all incoming rounds. I say again, log and record all incoming rounds.' The Motorola radio on my webbing squawks into life. 'Are you ready Cloonan?' It is the duty officer at Irishbatt HQ.

'Roger that,' I answer, 'Clonan on standby.' The disembodied voice up the hill in Irishbatt HQ issues what is known as a fragmentary warning order.

'Get yourselves ready now – there are casualties likely in Rshaf, Ayta Zutt, Bayt Yahun and Haddathah. Are you good to go? Over.' I reply in the affirmative. 'Wait out' is the reply. Then, just the hissing of the radio. Everyone in the Sisu is watching me. Even BS Begley. I'm in charge now. The lads are watching me closely, to get the measure of me. How I behave now, the orders I give, my command performance, will have consequences for all of us. I can either get it right now, or fuck it up for everyone around me. For keeps. No pressure.

The shelling rages around us for over an hour. Every few minutes, A Company troops fire red flares into the early morning light. This is by way of a formal agreement between the Israelis and the Irish. The flares are a mutually agreed warning signal indicating that direct hostile fire – intentional or otherwise – is impacting on our UN positions. The clattering of gunfire intensifies each time we send up a flare. 'They fuckin' know they're firing at us for fuck's sake!' shouts Corporal Kennedy over the noise. 'Stop givin them a fuckin reference point.'

By 7 AM the firing has ceased. The radio chatter dies down. The Motorola returns to life. 'Proceed to village of At Tiri. Bodies in the Wadi over.' Corporal Kennedy perks up immediately. 'You're gonna fuckin' love this, Sir.'

'Bodies in the Wadis' is Irishbatt shorthand for a retrieval operation. After attacks on the Israeli hilltop positions, the IDF sometimes allow for a short ceasefire in order that the bodies of dead Hizbullah fighters can be removed. The bodies are rarely intact. Usually a bit 'torn up', as Corporal Kennedy puts it, due to the sheer weight of fire directed down the slopes and avenues of approach to the firebases. Anyone caught in the open will draw fire – with catastrophic consequences. As we head for At Tiri, Corporal Kennedy fills me in on the gory details. 'If them bodies are out in the sun, Sir, they'll be fuckin cooked as well. Fuckin barbecued. All crispy and sometimes they're full of gas and ye cant get them into the body bags. And someone has to burst them with the bayonet, and let out the gas so they'll fit in. That's usually the officer's job.' Corporal Kennedy is rooting around the backpacks and he hands me a bayonet from his Steyr. BS Begley interrupts loudly. 'Put that back or I'll burst YOU with it.' Corporal Kennedy's cackling laughter recedes as he wriggles back into the hatch with his bayonet. I'm secretly relieved.

We get to Haddatthah en route to At Tiri. An officer from B Company is waiting near the graveyard at the edge of the village. There are a half-dozen or so women keening loudly and ululating over the deaths of two boys from Sidon. Their bodies are lying prone in a ditch just below DFF 17, Haddathah Compound. The infantry officer tells me that the area has been swept for booby traps. The ordnance officer – who deals with Improvised Explosive Devices or IEDs – has overseen an Engineers Specialist Search Team or ESST sweep of the track leading to the ditch. Captain Maguire – a Leitrim native – tells me that the Israelis have agreed that the bodies can be removed at 12.00. The wailing intensifies behind us. The women are joined by a group of men who direct hostile, angry looks towards us. Two medics from Battalion Headquarters join us in the Sisu.

At 12 PM, we move up the track. At the junction of the track and the ditch I dismount with BS Begley. We escort the medics up towards the two bodies. Both are intact. Both have been stripped of weapons and other equipment by the Israelis. One of the boys has had his trousers pulled down around his ankles. The blood on his exposed buttocks and genitalia has blackened in the heat. His legs are similarly bloodstained and blood has pooled and congealed around what remains of his trousers. His eyes are open. The other youth is lying on his back. His face has been blown off. I notice his hands. Small hands. Perfectly formed, unblemished by work or hard labour. Like a sculpture. The hands of an adolescent with his whole life in front of him.

The medics work in complete silence. I'm amazed at how gentle they are. They work as a team to heft the bodies into two body bags. As the zippers buzz shut, the relief is palpable. We scour around for personal effects. The bodies are stretchered back to the Sisu.

When we get back down to Haddathah the bodies are handed over.

The women are screaming. The BS mutters, 'Jesus, Mary and Joseph.'

We drive in silence all the way back to Al Yatun. I am sitting in the footwell of the Sisu writing a report as we head in. Corporal Kennedy is drinking coffee. His hands – calloused, with 'HATE' and 'LOVE' tattooed on his knuckles – are shaking.

# Chapter 11

# November

*78 Irishbatt Operations Summary November 1995*
*Shooting Incidents: 461, Firings Close to Irishbatt Positions: 50, Serious*
*Incidents involving armed elements: 23, Air Incursions by Israeli Aircraft: 14*
Unit History, 78 Irishbatt, UNIFIL

November opens with a bang. Literally. I am bounced out of my metal bed – hands clawing blindly at the mosquito net – by another attack on the compounds. This time – in retaliation for the deaths of the two boys from Sidon – Hizbullah attack DFF 23 or Charlie Compound overlooking the village of Brashit. It is 1.45 AM and the night sky is lit up with tracer rounds probing a 360-degree arc of fire from the Israeli firebase. They then open up with mortars and heavy machine gun fire. As I stagger out of the pre-fab the night is alive with cursing as the troops run for the bunkers. Green and red tracer rounds pulse across the horizon. Luminous necklaces of fire ripping into the sleeping villages and houses below. Gate 12 opens fire now. As I weave my way towards the operations room, I hear the whoosh of the incoming 155 shells. Then the earth shakes. The deafening roar of the high explosive rounds detonating around us. The red flares fly up from the roof. A tank round clips the water tower. The smack of the flat trajectory makes even the veterans cry out. 'Jazes.' Then Psycho announces over the PA – 'Wakey Wakey boys

86

and girls – Gate 12 has opened fire. Groundhog, Groundhog, Groundhog.' There is a chorus of abuse from the troops. The attack ends at 3 AM.

At 6 AM, a duty officer at Battalion Headquarters decides that it would be a good idea if I went on a 'recce' or reconnaissance patrol across all routes to assess the damage. I ask him across the Motorola if the routes have been cleared for mines or unexploded ordnance. 'Wait one,' he replies. 'Avoid Post 10 Alpha, Al Jurn. The guys there say there is a new rock in the roadway there. They don't like the look of it. Over.' It later turns out that the 'new rock' is in fact a roadside bomb. Placed there by the IDF. It is a hollow fibre glass device – indistinguishable from any other rock – containing 16.5kg of high explosives and ball bearings. I am told later by the ordnance officer that it detonates by proximity or by remote control. Thanks to the guys in 10 Alpha we narrowly avoid disaster. As we roll out the gate, I'm wondering how many other 'new rocks' might we encounter on this – or any other – patrol.

We turn left out of the checkpoint at Al Yatun and move up the hill to Tibnine. The village is deserted. We then turn right and move down into the wadi towards Ayta Zutt. As we descend into the wadi the air gets colder. Despite the sun peeping over the horizon. And I feel a strange vibration. Over and above the usual vibration from the diesel engine and the metal surfaces as we bounce down the track. Then there is a deafening roar. At eye level, to my right, I see an Israeli F16 fighter jet rising out of the wadi below us. The cockpit is a blur as it banks away from us and thunders up and out of the valley. I get the briefest impression of the Star of David on the fuselage. A split-second sequence. Sergeant Bracken pokes me in the back. 'That's an Airvirep. An Air Violation Report. You'd better call it in.' As I'm reaching for the Motorola and struggling to work out our grid coordinates, the radios whirr into life. As the Israeli jet passes through Irishbatt – the Observation Posts start calling in the overflight. There is another loud detonation over the ridgeline. 'Sonic boom,' says Sergeant Bracken. 'That fucker'll be havin' his breakfast in Haifa in a half an hour. Kosher.'

On return to Al Yatun, I'm informed that I have been detailed to supervise the 'Winterisation' of the post. With the nights growing colder, this means I must inspect the Damascus heaters that the troops have installed in all of their billets. These heaters are crude metal stoves that burn diesel on a drip-feed basis. To me they look like improvised explosive devices. But, somehow, they work and keep the prefabs warm without exploding or burning the place down. And miraculously no one dies of carbon monoxide poisoning. I do manage, however, to persuade battalion headquarters to give me a grant to buy smoke alarms. By the end of the first week of November, there is a smoke alarm installed in all of the billets. Sergeant Bracken reckons this will earn me some brownie points with the lads. 'That's the first good idea I've seen from an officer since we arrived in this shit-hole.' I find the faint praise disproportionately satisfying.

As a direct result of my display of initiative, the Battalion Executive Officer designates me 'Fire Safety Officer' for the Battalion. Apparently, when on patrols, I am to call into all of the posts and talk to the troops about fire safety and the dangers posed by carbon monoxide poisoning. Corporal Smith volunteers to assist me. He also comes up with a novel idea. He suggests that we demonstrate the danger of 'naked flames' in the pre-fabs – using a disused portakabin on the perimeter of the post. This particular – windowless – portakabin is scheduled for removal and refurbishment by a Polish maintenance company later in November. Corporal Smith suggests we assemble the troops and show them how quickly a fire can start in a portakabin. The idea being that we start a small fire in the portakabin and then demonstrate the fire-fighting characteristics of the different fire extinguishers – foam, powder, water and so on – to the troops.

This seems like a good idea. It also appeals to me as a way of passing an afternoon. I always loved starting fires as a kid. I put the idea to Commandant McManus. He suggests I do it on the day the Padre comes to hear confessions and say mass. 'That way you'll maximise your audience.'

Two days later, the Padre arrives on the post. We shepherd the troops of A Company and the BMR out to the perimeter fence. Corporal Smith is waiting with the fire extinguishers. I explain the hazards posed by smoking in the billets – especially given the wooden partitions and flammable, even explosive risks posed by the Damascus heaters. The A Company troops are getting bored and are shuffling about a bit. I decide to light our little fire. Corporal Smith has doused some of the floor with paraffin. I drop a match into a litter bin filled with paper. There is a blue flash and a sudden whoosh. Flames lick over the floor and run up the wall at amazing speed. There is an audible gasp of amazement from the troops who now start pushing their way out of the door.

Corporal Smith fumbles with the fire extinguisher. He breaks the seal on the water canister and points it 'at the base of the fire', as per the instructions on the label. A weak spout of water slops over the floor. The fire has now spread to the ceiling and flames are licking across the opposite wall. There are ominous cracks and bangs from the now burning floorboards under the bin. 'Abandon ship!' roars one of the troops. A melee ensues. The Padre leads the charge out of the door. I see several troops vault out the open windows. Myself and Corporal Smith fight a retreat out of the burning portakabin with the remaining extinguishers. The heat is intense and huge billows of smoke and flames flare up from the tinder-dry building. Within minutes the portakabin is burned to the

Blood, Sweat and Tears

ground. Black wisps of ash and other debris hang in the air. Corporal Smith's mouth hangs open in amazement. His glasses are completely fogged up.

I turn and see Commandant McManus and some of the infantry officers from A Company staring at the concrete base of the portakabin. It is all that remains.

I am subsequently relieved of my duties as Fire Safety Officer. However, the troops unanimously agree that it was the most impressive demonstration of the dangers of fire and smoke inhalation that they have ever seen. 'Fair play to ye, Sir.' They never tire of reminding me of the day I 'burnt down the gaff.' 'Ye really burnt the fuck out of it.' The battalion logs staff however, did order new fire extinguishers for all the posts. The Padre had remarked that his Holy Water bottle would have been more effective on the blaze than the ancient UN fire extinguishers. So our demonstration wasn't totally in vain.

A couple of days later I am designated Entertainments Officer for Al Yatun. BS Begley reassures me on this detail. 'Just make sure there is no fighting at the bingo on a Friday night. And make sure there is a film every Saturday night in the canteen. Simple.' Corporal Kennedy chimes in in agreement. 'Yeah, not even an officer could fuck that up.'

'Bingo', I discover, loosely describes what passes for entertainment on Friday nights in Al Yatun. Those personnel not on duty are permitted to attend Bingo in the canteen or 'canner' where they can consume a maximum of four cans of Heineken. There are no spirits permitted and the four can rule is supposed to be rigorously enforced. So, on the first Friday in November – with the entire camp bathed in diesel fumes – I enter the smoky fug of the canteen to monitor events with Sergeant Bracken and Corporal Kennedy as my bodyguards. The canteen is heaving with troops. Everyone is wearing parka jackets despite the heat. Faces are lit up

90

with drink. I suspect the four can rule is not being enforced. And there is a frenzied atmosphere.

A senior NCO from A Company waddles up to the stage in his oversized parka and bangs on the wall with a stick. Silence falls in the room and he commences proceedings. 'Right. Ye'll have yer fuckin' pencils ready. So you will. And, here we have it. Two fat ladies . . . Six.' All hell breaks loose. One NCO – whose nickname I learn is Sergeant Fuckin-Fuck in recognition of his prowess at swearing – is screaming loudly in protest. 'Two fuckin' fat ladies? I fuckin' marked the wrong fuckin' number ye fucker ye.'

'Too fuckin' bad. That's your own look out so it is,' is the reply.

The fight starts almost immediately. Sergeant Bracken grabs me by the scruff of the neck and drags me outside into the cold night air. 'Ehh, I wouldn't stay in there if I was you.' I hear Corporal Kennedy shouting inside, 'Stay down ye fucker ye.' Order is eventually restored. Bingo in the Leb however, is somewhat different to that genteel – if undemanding – entertainment I had previously associated with elderly ladies back in Ireland. Somehow, however, Lebanese Bingo – or as the lads refer to it, 'no-holds-barred Bingo' – is extremely popular with the troops.

That night I get my weekly phone call to Ireland. My Mum answers the phone.

'How are you getting on my love?' she asks.

'Ehh, I was at the bingo tonight.'

'Oh, that sounds lovely.' We are separated by more than distance. I am homesick.

The following night I organise the film night in Al Yatun. I send BS Begley down to Battalion Headquarters to get a suitable video. I trust his judgement and feel he will have a better handle than me on what will play well with the troops. By 8 PM the canteen is once again heaving with parka-clad troops. Faces luminous with alcohol and feverish expectation. A large screen has been erected by Sergeant Fuckin-Fuck and some other foul-mouthed individual. The canteen falls silent as myself and BS Begley arrive with the video. Sergeant Fuckin-Fuck slaps the video into the player and turns off the lights.

The opening frames of Disney's *The Lion King* flicker on to the screen. Pandemonium ensues. A roar of indignation erupts from the troops. Cans and other missiles are hurled at the screen. Sergeant Fuckin-Fuck leaps out in front of the screen – his shadow ridiculously large behind him. 'Ye shower of fuckin' ungrateful fuckin' bollixes!' he roars. 'Ye'll fuckin' watch what yer fuckin' given so you will.' This declaration and the threat 'to close the fuckin' bar' leads to a sullen, tense silence. *The Lion King* continues amid much mutinous muttering. Eventually, though, the room falls completely silent. After one and a half hours of rapt attention – as Simba lifts the lion cub triumphantly in the air – the troops erupt in wild cheering. 'Go on ye fuckin' good thing ye' is the general consensus. 'Hakuna Matata' becomes the universal greeting in Al Yatun. And thankfully comes to replace 'Mary Robinson wears no knickers' as the universal greeting to the Irish in the neighbouring battalion areas.

# Chapter 12

# I Am Secret Man

*Lift your eyes with hope, not through the rifle sights
sing a song for love, and not for wars.*

Words of 'Shir LaShalom' ('Song for Peace'), read by
Yithzhak Rabin as he was assassinated in November 1995

On the Sunday night – directly after our screening of *The Lion King*, I am rostered as patrol officer. At 2 AM, as we come back to Al Yatun after a patrol, there is a commotion at the entrance to the post. There is a car blocking access to the post and we cannot get the Sisus in the gate. The duty sergeant from A Company is standing in the checkpoint as there is a standoff developing. As we rev up the engines impatiently I can see a large black Mercedes halted between the tank stops, slap-bang in the middle of the checkpoint. I glance up on the roof and note that the A Company troops have the general purpose machine gun trained on the vehicle. That's somewhat reassuring. The lads in the sandbagged position on the roof give me the thumbs up. 'Hakuna Matata' they call softly down to me. They are delighted at their sense of humour. I disconnect the headset and hop down to investigate.

The corporal on the checkpoint nods at me and points to the rear window of the Mercedes. The windows are heavily tinted and blacked out. I cannot see into the car despite the searchlight trained directly at it.

The electric rear windows hum as they are lowered from within. I look inside and see a young man on the back seat dressed in a very sharp suit. Shirt and tie. Cufflinks. And, oddly, a pair of wraparound sunglasses. He has an AK-47 across his lap. It is just resting there. At least he's not pointing it at me. And he's smiling broadly at me. '*Ahlan wa sahlan*.' We exchange greetings. 'What is the problem with these men, Lieutenant?' he asks. 'Why can I not go into the village?' I inform him that he cannot proceed with the assault rifle. That he must surrender it to us before he goes into the village. He pulls the sunglasses down over the bridge of his nose and, looking conspiratorially at me, motions for me to come closer. I lean a little into the window. To be honest, I'm a bit nervous now.

'But, Lieutenant, I cannot give you the gun. Because.' He looks around carefully to ensure he cannot be overheard. 'Because, I am secret man. Like James Bond.' Eventually we persuade 007 to turn around and head back to wherever he came from. The village of Haris can sleep soundly – safe in the knowledge that on at least this one occasion we've managed to repel the mysterious 'secret man'. Hell-bent on who knows what.

On the Monday morning, news filters through to us that Yithzhak Rabin has been assassinated in Tel Aviv. Gunned down in the Kings of Israel Square by Yigal Amir. Apparently he has been shot for his part in the negotiation and signature of the Oslo Peace Accords. The incident is sobering. Tension seems to be mounting throughout the region on a number of fronts. Hizbullah are certainly increasing their attacks on the Israeli positions within our area.

On Thursday night, 9 November, Hizbullah unleash a prolonged, coordinated attack on DFF 20A overlooking Bayt Yahun. They simultaneously attack DFF 23 – Brashit Compound – overlooking C Company Headquarters. We watch from Al Yatun as Hizbullah try to take the hilltop forts. They move forward in classic fire and manoeuvre tactics. We cannot see individuals, but we can see the exchange of red and green tracer fire as they slowly approach the outer perimeters of the compounds. The fire on both sides intensifies. The radios are chattering away, reporting each mortar round, each salvo of shells lobbed into the Irish Battalion area from Gates 12 and 14A. The firefight rages for an hour or two and then subsides around midnight.

The following morning, at 5.01 AM, Hizbullah launch fresh attacks on the same compounds. The fighting continues all morning. There are more bodies in the wadis. The local Red Crescent ambulance crews are terrified. They are afraid to approach the outer slopes of the compounds for fear of hostile fire. The BMR is again tasked with recovery of the bodies. We get used to the routine. Collecting the remains. Watching the medics bagging and tagging them. Handing them over to the families at Tibnine Hospital. The female relatives weeping inconsolably. The male relatives glaring at us with outright hostility. We hear that there are casualties on the Israeli side also. Hizbullah boast that they are inflicting a like number of casualties on the IDF. The military refer to it as a '1 to 1 exchange ratio'. Somewhere in Israel, a family is receiving word of the death of a son, in some unknown location in Lebanon. None of this makes the news in Ireland.

To us, the assaults on the compounds by Hizbullah appear suicidal. With little or no chance of breaching the defences of the firebases, it is a war of attrition. The Hizbullah fighters invariably end up in the wadis. Dismembered by fire. Disfigured. The number of martyr posters increases in the villages and along the roads leading into Tyre and Sidon. The number of villagers killed and injured in the crossfire also increases daily. By the end of November, Hizbullah are launching major attacks throughout Irishbatt's AO – on average, one attack every seventy-two hours.

In the meantime, the routine associated with Irishbatt's deployment continues apace. Each morning the water trucks deliver drinking water to the UN posts and checkpoints. The so-called 'Honey Wagons' pump the sewage out of our septic tanks. When the Honey Wagon is grounded because of fighting in the AO, the smell of human shit intensifies around our positions. And to add insult to injury, when this happens there is usually no water re-supply either. Psycho dolefully announces water rationing over the PA system. '*Éist le seo* – All personnel on Al Ya Gloom be advised, no showers permitted.' Followed by a falsetto 'Get me off this fuckin' rock.'

Throughout this period of heightened tension, the BMR continues its patrol routine. The days are blurring into night. I don't like the night patrols. Especially between midnight and 6 AM. Because that's when most of the Hizbullah attacks take place. It feels like a game of high stakes poker. Sometimes, up on the back hatch of the Sisu, patrolling at night, I mull over what might happen if we are within range of a compound when it gets hit up by Hizbullah. We'd definitely be in the crossfire. Particularly as neither side pays any particular heed to civilian casualties, or UN casualties for that matter. From our briefings, I am aware that precisely 50 percent of Irish casualties are inflicted by Hizbullah and 50 percent by the Israelis and their proxies. We are the meat in the sandwich. A thin green line of Irish troops.

The Israeli firebases also play mind games with us. They constantly track us with their weapon systems as we patrol beneath them. We watch as their weapons traverse in bearing and elevation. Slowly and deliberately keeping us in their sights whenever we are within range. This concentrates the mind somewhat. Knowing that at any moment they are capable of opening fire indiscriminately. And having been in the wadis – collecting the dismembered and mutilated – we know exactly the effect of that indiscriminate fire. Our 20mm armour is of little protection. Our flak jackets and helmets even less so. 'Our costumes' as Corporal Kennedy refers to them.

At night, when we approach the firebases along rutted tracks the Israelis engage in a number of psychological games with us. Sometimes they will fire a burst of machine gun close to us. Tracers buzzing by with metres to spare. As the patrol commander, with head, shoulders and chest out of the observation hatch, this is an uncomfortable experience to say the least. When it happens a few times, I resort to repeating 'fuck it, fuck it, fuck it' over and over, a foul-mouthed Rosary. At other times, the Israelis direct powerful searchlights at us, blinding the driver. Forcing us to turn off night vision equipment.

The occupants of the Cuckoo's Nest – or DFF 13 – are particularly vindictive. They like to intimidate the UN whenever possible and regularly send up flares and other ordnance as we patrol the road from Haddathah to Rshaf. It is a long, narrow, straight track leading from Haddathah to Rshaf. There is a steep drop on either side of the road. Nowhere to turn. Nowhere to hide. Once on that track, we are fully committed to continuing right to the perimeter of the Cuckoo's Nest in order to make a three-point turn on a gravel and sand layby. And then the long trek back, constantly monitoring the firebase for signs of hostile activity.

We do this night after night after night. Hundreds of times. By the same token, by mid November, I've seen the Cuckoo's Nest explode into action – pumping thousands of high velocity shells into the area around it. Indiscriminate fire. Lethal fire. In a full 360-degree arc, without warning. A Lottery. Each time we approach it on patrol, I hold my breath. Watching it gradually loom larger as we approach along the track. Staring up at its ramparts as we turn beneath it. Watching it recede into the darkness as we move back towards B Company Headquarters at 6-38. At any moment expecting it to erupt. To rain heavy fire down on us. I don't want to end up like the two boys from Sidon. I'm trying very hard to turn down the volume on these disturbing, unsettling thoughts.

So, each time we make that approach, I think of my parents at home. I think of them sleeping. I say the Hail Mary. Over and over. Even though I'm not really sure about God. It's a habit from school. That's what I tell myself. I also notice that the guys in the Sisu are tense as well. And, as time wears on, they begin looking to me for reassurance. Even the old sweats like Corporal Kennedy. Even BS Begley. They constantly glance over at me in the green-lit interior of the Sisu. Reading my face for signs of alarm, fear, stupidity, whatever. I am acquiring a poker face. For patrols, for shelling, for the random but increasingly frequent – and increasingly violent – attacks.

And when I'm on down time, I find I'm hitting the bottle that bit harder. Drinking anything and everything that bit faster. 'Get it into ye,' as Corporal Kennedy says. To take the edge off things. To take the edge off the long dark nights in Lebanon. We have just two CDs in our makeshift bar. Elvis Presley's Greatest Hits and Frank Sinatra Sings Cole Porter. And as we listen to Elvis and Sinatra, over and over again, we drink Bottles of Chateau Musar, Kefraya. And whiskey. The amber lady putting us to sleep and wrapping us up in her tender, fiery embrace. No one else loves us here.

By day though, Irishbatt's day-to-day routines are evolving at their own pace – irrespective of the nighttime attacks and the recurring dawn chorus of morning assaults. The battalion commander has even begun his inspection regime. During the six-month deployment, OC Irishbatt – we are informed – will visit us on at least three separate occasions to inspect our posts. The interpersonal chemistry and power dynamics between those senior officers posted to Battalion Headquarters play a pivotal role in determining the atmosphere within any Irish deployment on UN service. With each deployment overseas, a collective personality emerges among those staff officers at Battalion Headquarters. As a consequence, each battalion has its own unique identity. The personal idiosyncrasies, motivations, and peccadilloes of senior officers determine the atmosphere for the 600 or so Irish troops within each battalion. With mixed results. Some battalions are dysfunctional, stressful workplace environments. Some are harmonious.

The troops refer to this phenomenon in two ways. A happy battalion staff presides over a 'Happy Batt'. A battalion staff with a lack of personality, charisma or plain common sense presides over what is known as a 'Sad Batt'. Fortunately for us, ours is a reasonably happy battalion. As a junior officer however, I have learned to avoid Camp Shamrock and the Battalion Headquarters as much as is humanly possible. Unfortunately for me, I have to attend regular briefings there. Usually in the Operations bunker, a subterranean reinforced concrete bunker that constantly smells of damp. An artificially-lit underworld occupied by the senior officers of Battalion Headquarters. Most of whom are good men and women. Some of them are exceptionally good officers. There are however, one or two narcissistic and rather unpleasant senior officers who inhabit Camp Shamrock. They stalk its environs like two ageing dinosaurs. We call them the 'purple people eaters'.

One day, as we are refuelling in Camp Shamrock, Sergeant Bracken observes one of them – Commandant Molloy – walking along with a swagger stick of all things. No doubt, looking for someone to persecute. Sergeant Bracken nudges me and points at Commandant Molloy and whispers in his Kildare accent, 'Once a fighting cock – now a feather duster.' We have a laugh at his expense. Molloy eyes me suspiciously from the distance and begins to walk toward us. Happily, the driver revs up the engines and we are gone in cloud of black smoke before he reaches us.

After six weeks in the AO, it becomes clearer and clearer to me that Commandant Molloy has taken a particular dislike to me. Back in Al Yatun, I ask Commandant McManus for some advice on how to deal with this issue. He laughs and tells me that, 'Unfortunately, Molloy tends not to like people he knows. Don't take it personally, just stay out of his orbit. Keep off his radar. He's got too much time on his hands.' So I'll just have to stay out of his way – because, when you are deployed overseas in such circumstances – answerable to a senior officer such as him – there is no escape. No going home. You are a guest of the Irish Army, 24/7, 7/7 for 200 days.

# Chapter 13

# Cockroach Hall

*Better than coffee fucking*

In the third week of November – between attacks and the inevitable collection of bodies from the wadis – the battalion commander schedules his first inspection of Al Yatun. Those not on duty or patrol form up on parade in ridiculous blue cravats and berets awaiting his arrival. Lieutenant Colonel Duff arrives and duly inspects those of us present. He then tours the post, visiting the cookhouse, canteen, operations cell, communications centre and sleeping accommodation. After, we retire to the officer's mess for coffee. Accompanied by his retinue of staff officers and the battalion sergeant major. So far, so painless.

At this point, Commandant McManus is due to give an overview of the A Company area of operations. The centrepiece of this briefing focuses around a large map of the area which is contained within a special wooden cabinet mounted on the wall of the mess. Mac opens the doors of the cabinet with a flourish. Unfortunately, however, the map has been shredded by a mouse. Or mice. One of whom hops out and scurries across the floor. Our VIP guests are not amused.

Two days later we are informed that Al Yatun is to be subjected to a rigorous health and hygiene audit. A senior officer from the Polish medical company based at UNIFIL HQ in Naqoura will be arriving to conduct the inspection. The Polish medical officer duly arrives into Al Yatun. He is remarkably young-looking for a medical officer and he appears a little nervous. Particularly when Psycho announces his arrival over the tannoy. 'Attention all personnel – make sure you have clean jocks on ye – the Doctor is here.'

Dr Ostrowska – or Yashek – is blonde and blue-eyed. He has never been outside of UNIFIL Headquarters at Naqoura and is nervous. He asks us about the likelihood of a Hizbullah attack. When we show him the bullet holes in the gabions and blast walls he visibly blanches. 'OK – I get this over with as quick as possible. You have problem with feral cats, mice, rats and cockroaches?' Obviously the story of the mouse in the map cabinet has grown legs.

Major Yashek starts his rounds. We are surprised at his thoroughness. He starts on the roof and requisitions field dressings and trauma kits for each of our observation posts. He visits the latrines and shower blocks and declares them 'unfit for human habitation'. We are delighted. The engineers are pissed off as they have to dig a new septic tank. Deeper than before. Yashek is also horrified by our cookhouse. It is built with hollow blocks and has become hopelessly infested with cockroaches. We call it Cockroach Hall. Cockroaches crawl the walls and ceiling. Whole family groups of cockroaches promenade freely across every surface. Cockroaches traverse the floor and food preparation areas and crawl in and out of the toasters by the breakfast area. Yashek is speechless. Pops, the cook, attempts to emphasise the gravity of the situation by announcing – in all seriousness – 'They're comin' out in their fuckin' drones sir. In their fuckin drones.'

'You mean "droves",' corrects Yashek. Pops eyes him poisonously. Yashek continues, 'Are these eggs the best you are doing for the men?'

'I only cook them eggs, Sir,' replies Pops, cigarette dangling from his mouth, 'I don't fuckin' lay them.'

The cookhouse is declared unfit for human habitation. In the meantime, we have set up a temporary clinic in the canteen. The troops line up and Yashek examines everyone. Constantly glancing at his watch. The lads torment him with symptoms. Some have brought the 'fatbuster' tablets from Hafif's shop and are complaining loudly about flatulence and weight gain. Yashek is clearly flustered. Nonetheless, he is thorough. Sergeant Fuckin-Fuck tells him he is suffering from mouth ulcers. Yashek is concerned and shines a torch into his mouth. He asks, 'Have you ulceration of any other soft tissues?' Sergeant Fuckin-Fuck hesitates and replies, 'I don't use tissues on em – just fuckin' Bonjela.' Yashek looks concerned and asks Sergeant Fuckin-Fuck to remove his trousers. He then gets him to bend over and shines a penlight up his anus. 'To check for further ulceration.' The troops queuing at the door are spooked by this. Not party to Sergeant Fuckin-Fuck's conversation with Yashek, they begin whispering to one another. Eventually word gets out from the queue that the Polish doctor is 'shinin' a torch up everyone's hole.' Even Psycho is spooked.

It is getting dark when Yashek is finishing his rounds. His driver is impatiently waiting for him in the vehicle park – flak jacket and helmet in hand. We are shaking hands with Yashek, who promises reports in due course. Then DFF 17 in Bayt Yahun opens up. Psycho sings out his announcements. 'Attention all personnel – Gate 12 has opened fire.' Yashek's face is contorted with fear. His blue eyes roll a little and I feel sorry for him. We get him into the officer's mess. Down on the floor behind the bar. We give him a shot of Jagermeister to calm his nerves. With each heavy thud outside, flecks of whitewash and dust puff from the walls of the bar. The shells are adjusting closer to Al Yatun. The thuds grow louder – now with a clearly audible whistle. Just like the movies. Just like the noises and sound effects I used to make with my Airfix toy soldiers when I was a kid. Suddenly the building rocks. There is also a sudden change in air pressure. The Perspex windows are catapulted out of their frames with a massive thunderclap. I find myself crawling in under the sink of the bar – squeezing in between the fridge and the wall for some reason. I manage to pull myself together. Yashek is rocking forward and back on his heels holding his head in his hands. Psycho bursts in. 'Did ye fuckin' hear that one?' Psycho seems elated. 'Up the fuckin' Dubs!' he shouts. He then disappears back into the Communications Centre.

The thudding shells veer south of our position and pound the village of Haris. I see Hafif scurrying past the now open window towards the bunker. With his precious IOU ledger and a large bag – presumably stuffed with dollars. Yashek is muttering in Polish. I pour him another Jagermeister. And another. After a while, when things have settled down, we are joined by Commandant McManus and one of the infantry officers from A Company. Everyone is covered in white dust. We retire to the roof and watch the dying firefight over a bottle of Jameson and the last of the Jagermeister, which tastes like perfume. Yashek takes everyone's blood pressure. We are all suffering from hypertension it seems. The all-clear sounds and we see a vehicle careering up the hill from Tibnine towards the checkpoint. As it gets closer we notice the UN markings and the Irish pennant. 'Aha,' says Mac. 'If it isn't the Battalion Commander coming up to tuck us all in.' We all find this remarkably funny for some reason and are laughing ourselves sick as the jeep rolls across the cattle grid and rumble strips into the vehicle park. The Battalion Chaplain – Fr Ryan – emerges wearing a flak jacket and helmet. 'Fucking hell, it's the Padre.'

Fr Ryan is laughing as he emerges out onto the roof. Down below Psycho has announced 'Attention all personnel, the battalion druid has arrived on post.' He scans the roof and takes in the bottles and glassy-eyed looks. 'A sundowner at sunset?' he asks. 'Better than coffee fucking,' replies Yashek, who doesn't seem to realise that Fr Ryan is the Padre. The Padre, tactfully, carefully corrects his syntax. 'I think you mean to say, better ... than ... fucking ... coffee.' That breaks the tension and he joins us for a drink. We are wary of the Padre as he is a highly observant individual with a sharp wit – and, most of all, capable of drinking each and every one of us under the table.

Fr Ryan waxes lyrical. He is holding his Jameson up to the glare of the searchlight pointing down at the checkpoint. 'You know, torture isn't necessary in order to get inside someone's head.' Yashek looks alarmed. 'Pour in the drink, and most men pour out their hearts. A good priest engages with the troops – even the hardest nuts. Peels back the layers, like an onion.' He looks at each of us in turn with a beatific smile. We are gathering our thoughts, hoping to change the subject when suddenly Yashek bursts into tears. He is definitely the worse for wear. Between anguished sobs he blurts, 'I am not even doctor. I am NOT knowing why Colonel Doctor Zaleski is sending me here to the hills. He says hospital doctors in Naqoura are too busy for the stupid inspection in the hills. He says he is sending me – pest controlling officer – because the Paddies is not asking too many questions.'

Fr Ryan raises an eyebrow and gives each of us in turn a smile. 'Now, now Yashek. Major Ostrowska. Not a doctor? Surely you have some medical training?' I'm thinking about Sergeant Fuckin-Fuck and the torchlight inspection of his backside.

Yashek replies energetically, 'Well, of course, somehow. I am Veterinarian. Graduate of Warsava University of Life Sciences. Ursynow.'

We are somewhat relieved. Mac saves his blushes.

'Yashek. That's even better than a doctor. I mean, you have to know about all sorts. Cats, cows, birds. Humans are simple. Just two models. Man, woman. You did a great job in Al Yatun today. Even cured Sergeant Fuckin-Fuck's mouth ulcers.' We are in stitches at this point. Even Yashek seems more sure of himself. Yashek's driver is down in the vehicle park staring up at the roof. Time to go. Fr Ryan reassures him as we retrieve his flak jacket and helmet from the bar. 'Don't worry, Major Ostrowska. Your secret is safe with us. Consider it as though uttered within the seal of the confessional.' Yashek shakes hands with each of us several times. He won't forget Al Yatun for a long time. We are all slightly in awe of the Padre. And I think that Yashek is precisely the type of vet that might just make it into the *Readers Digest* some day.

# Chapter 14

# Ten out of Ten

*If I am kill you. If I kill Irish. Then eight out of ten for Allah.*

The last week of November begins eventfully. There are violent thunderstorms throughout Irishbatt with heavy rain and hail. Patrolling at night becomes even more entertaining. Perched high on the rear of the Sisu – a metal perch, I hasten to add – I am surrounded by whiplash aerials and a serrated metal upright which serves to cut overhead wires in order to avoid decapitation by low-hanging cables. Lightning conductors all. As bolt lightning smashes into the ground about us and fork lightning strikes satellite dishes and metal stovepipes all around us – I am tempted to close the hatch and lie down in the footwell of the APC. But the roads and tracks – particularly around the steep-edged wadis – are beginning to subside. All eyes are needed up top to navigate the slippery tracks. As Sergeant Bracken puts it, 'If we slide down into the wadi, we'll start to tumble. And we'll be like baked beans in here when they pull us out. So. You can get the head taken off ye with lightning or take your chances with the cliffs. Your call, Sir. No stress. It's called Catch-22, I think.'

The weather improves however and the morning of 28 November brings sunshine once more. That's when the rear observation post at Al Yatun catch sight of some suspicious movement to our rear. Down by an abandoned quarry called the Stone Crusher we see a number of men moving around the abandoned outhouses. They are armed. At least one is carrying an RPG or Rocket Propelled Grenade. Myself and Commandant McManus climb the back post and watch the activity through binoculars. One of the men is sneaking – quite theatrically, like Wile E. Coyote in *Looney Tunes* – around the piles of stone and sand. RPG in hand. Mac looks at me and sighs. 'You'll need to go down and see what those clowns are up to. Make sure they can see you coming. Don't surprise them. They look a bit fidgety.'

So. Myself and BS Begley roll out the gate and down the dusty track to the rear of the post. We're happy enough to take this route as it has been traversed all day by ancient battered Mercedes cars and trucks. We should be OK. With a large plume of dust announcing our arrival, we come to a halt 100 metres or so short of the Stone Crusher. I cannot see anyone. I wriggle out of the hatch, disconnect the headset and clamber down the side of the vehicle. BS Begley does the same and we walk up towards the outhouses. I'm starting to sweat a bit. The BS shouts out a greeting in Arabic, '*Ahlan wa sahlan.*' He winks at me as two skinny youths emerge from the outhouses. Their weapons are pointed down at the dusty brown earth. One has the straggly beginnings of a beard. The other only wisps of hair on his cheeks and chin. I think of the bodies of the two boys from Sidon. The bearded wonder is first to speak. 'Kifak Irish.' He returns our greeting and grins sheepishly at us. BS Begley has slung his Steyr rifle over his back and has thrust his hand out. The boys shake hands with us. This requires the bearded one to lay the RPG on the ground. BS Begley deftly places his boot across the stock, pinning it firmly on the ground.

The bearded one – Ramzi – gets a little excited. 'That is for shoot the bird!' he exclaims.

'And what kind of bird were you hoping to shoot with a 1 kilo war-head?' asks Begley. 'Big bird. Ehh, Bagaa. Not farouge or chicken. Ehh, swan thing.' He scoops up the RPG. 'We'll have to take that. I'm sorry. But there'd be nothing left of a swan if you hit him with this yoke. You'd be better off strangling him.' The boys are visibly upset and Ramzi gives me the evil eye. I ask him what he thinks his chances are if he runs up to the Cuckoo's Nest with the RPG. 'If I am go to God and try to kill Israeli then that is good. Try to kill Israeli is ten out of ten for Allah'

'And what if you kill me?' I ask him. Ramzi thinks about this for a second. Then, looking me in the eyes, he replies. 'If I am kill you. If I kill Irish. Then eight out of ten for Allah.' I am somewhat discouraged by his honesty.

We have averted an attack. We have possibly saved a life. On the way back to Al Yatun the BS tells me that I am bringing peace to the Middle East. 'Little by little, bit by bit.' Corporal Burke sings 'One Day at a Time, Sweet Jesus', in his Donegal accent. I notice that he never gets out of the Sisu. He is always quiet on patrol and has become quite subdued in general.

When we get back to Al Yatun, we report the incident over the land-line to Operations. The duty officer asks me how to spell *Bagaa*.

The following morning – the last day of November – we are rudely awakened at 5 AM. Hizbullah have launched a major attack on DFF 17 overlooking Haddathah. The Israeli retaliation is swift and overwhelming. The Hizbullah attack withers under the weight of concentrated artillery fire from Gates 12 and 14. The Israelis also launch a number of air assaults. Corporal Kennedy pointing skyward. 'Can you see it. Can ye see the fucker, look it's a speck.' And then the roar of the F16 thundering low, flying by contour into Haddathah and releasing its payload of 500lb bombs. The sonic boom as it echoes over the ridgeline, seconds later back in Israeli airspace. All the while another F16, circling a little higher, providing top cover for his buddy.

When the Hizbullah attack has ceased entirely, the Israelis continue to fire sporadically. We watch as a small group of Israeli troops exits Haddathah compound and moves down the slope. Gingerly, slowly. One of the troops carrying a 77 set – just like our own. Ahead of them a German Shepherd pausing, sniffing the air and then rushing forward in bounds. They disappear into the olive groves at the base of the hill. Then we hear the sharp staccato of automatic gunfire. Seconds later, two Apache Helicopter Gunships buzz and clatter over the ridgeline and move into a holding pattern over Haddathah. Both are pumping out flares and chaff to deter missile attacks from below. They are providing cover for the Israeli troops now retreating with the dog into the compound. One of the choppers swoops low and begins to fire into a house at the edge of Haddathah. Firing the chain-gun slung beneath its nose directly into the house below. There is a loud buzzing noise as the weapon is fired. The chopper then hovers slowly up the line of detached houses.

We can hear the register of the helicopter's engine clearly. A loud clattering with a lower tone of torque being applied as the tail lifts – like some stinging insect – and the cockpit and weapon are again aimed at another household. More buzzing as roof tiles, windows, masonry, disintegrate under the hail of point-five rounds. The tracer rounds burning and smouldering. Some ricochet and whine off in all directions. I'm wondering now about all of the children I see in Haddathah. The ones who run alongside us. The ones I see playing in the gardens of these very houses. Where are they now? What is happening to the little ones? A loud bark then as a TOW missile is fired. Point blank into the house. The house collapses in on top of itself. Then more loud barks as other TOW missiles are fired at point blank range. The wire-guided missiles leave behind them a gossamer pattern of discarded metal filaments. Lying like spider webs across the gutters and rooftops of the destroyed houses. Silent testimony to human ingenuity. Testimony to our propensity for violence. Smart weapons. Dumb dead in the rubble.

The choppers circle lazily, gaining height with white-hot flares detonating every two to three seconds. They disappear over the ridge. Then total silence. Later that afternoon, we collect the bodies from the olive grove at the base of the hill. Over the call to prayer from the Mosque in Haddathah I am straining to listen to the radio traffic. I see the now familiar sight of the Red Crescent ambulance approaching from Ayta az Zutt. Sirens blaring. Lights flashing. Ready to take more bodies to the morgue in Tibnine Hospital.

As the burned and blackened bodies are hefted into the back of the ambulance I recognise Ramzi's scraggly beard among the lifeless lolling heads. He got his ten out of ten it would seem.

# Chapter 15

# December

*78 Irishbatt Operations Summary December 1995*
*Shooting Incidents: 138, Firings Close to Irishbatt Positions: 2, Serious Incidents*
*involving armed elements: 16, Air Incursions by Israeli Aircraft: 7*

Unit History, 78 Irishbatt, UNIFIL

December sees temperatures plummet in the AO. I had always associated Lebanon and the Middle East with childhood images of camels and rolling desert sands. Oases shaded with palm trees. The topography in Irishbatt however is a rocky, hilly landscape. Towering ridgelines and steep wadis. A snow-covered Mount Hermon and the Golan Heights to the north and east. The Israeli border, purple glowing ridgelines and endless olive groves and vineyards to the south. In many respects, Irishbatt's AO is reminiscent of a barren, rocky Burren. Browner than Ireland perhaps. Less green. A little harsher – the contours sharp and less rounded than those at home. The contrasts between ridgeline and wadi in Lebanon sharper than drumlin and gentle-sloped valley at home.

What surprises me is the frost. Because of the lack of moisture in the air, the frost is invisible. There is no tell-tale white frost as at home. Hands stick to the metal surfaces of the Sisus in the morning.

My contact with home is sporadic. My Mum writes to me each week. She tells me about the goings on at home. It all seems very far away. My father scribbles a short note occasionally. I have received just one letter so far from my girlfriend. I read it and re-read it. She says that she is 'very busy'. I carry it around with me. I find I'm homesick or something. A new experience for me. I keep trying to write a letter explaining this. But I cant. I'm not even sure who to write to. I definitely feel sore at heart, homesick and, well, lonely. I'm mystified by this curious set of emotions.

The mail is brought up from Camp Shamrock every couple of days. Psycho's announcement of '*Éist le seo* [Listen to this] – Attention all personnel. Get your Dear John letters. Hankies available from the CS.' The troops converge on the Communications Centre. This is the great leveller. The brutal and licentious are transformed into schoolboys at the prospect of a letter from home. The harsh façade of hard faces, tattoos and uniforms is momentarily lifted. From the most hardened and cynical old sweats to the most innocent first-timers, all let their guard slip and rush unselfconsciously to the Communications Centre. They anxiously scan the piles of letters arranged in alphabetical order. Letters are passed back along the line until all have been distributed.

Eventually, the crowd thins until all that remains are those for whom there is no post. They hang around for a bit, then shrug it off and trudge back to the billets. If you look carefully, you can detect a slight, almost imperceptible, stoop in the shoulders. Eyes fixed firmly on some spot on the ground. Even the hardest cases. Everyone – without exception – is lonely. Everyone at some point experiences the disappointment of not getting a letter from home. Some of the troops get no letters throughout the entire deployment. Usually older guys. Separated. Estranged.

Those that get letters find a silent place and are lost in the words from home. Sometimes there is bad news.

During the first week of December, Sergeant Fuckin-Fuck from A Company gets a letter from his wife saying that she has left him. For good this time. Dumped all of his clothes outside his mother's house in Cabra. He manages to bottle it up for most of the day. Then, that night, he runs out to the checkpoint. Discarding his flak jacket and weapon on the way. Screaming for a taxi to take him to Beirut. So that he can fly home. It takes half a dozen men to subdue him. Sergeant Fuckin-Fuck, despite his small stature, has the strength of ten men in his blind rage and grief. He is incoherent and literally howls at the moon over Al Yatun. He eventually goes quiet, then slumps, sobbing uncontrollably. Two or three NCOs from A Company manhandle him into a billet. Their hard faces are distraught. This is one of the worst things that can happen overseas. So far from home. No control. By the end of the week, Sergeant Fuckin-Fuck has returned to normal again. No one makes any reference to his wife and daughter. BS Begley tells me that his only daughter is doing her Leaving Certificate this year and that his wife has had enough of Sergeant Fuckin-Fuck. 'He'd be hard going, I'd say,' observes the BS.

Meanwhile, I am summoned by the Battalion Executive Officer to Camp Shamrock for an 'urgent word'. I hitch a ride down to Shamrock with Commandant McManus who is attending a briefing. We are hunched over in the back of a Toyota jeep in our flak jackets and helmets. Mac observes that I haven't quite been myself of late. He asks me if everything is OK. I tell him about the letter – the one and only letter – from my girlfriend. Mac looks at me and announces, 'You're finished Clonan. Finished. Make sure you send me an invite to the wedding.' As we part company outside the Operations Bunker his laughter – and those prophetic words – are ringing in my ears.

The Battalion Executive Officer's office is located to the rear of the Battalion's administrative centre. This is where the Battalion Sergeant Major is to be found. He spots me entering the office. 'AHA LIEU-TENANT CLOONAN. WE'VE BEEN EXPECTING YOU.' This makes me a bit nervous as he ushers me into Commandant Evans's office. Commandant Evans looks up briefly and motions for me to sit. An encouraging sign. After a while he finishes scratching his signature on documents and straightens up. Clearing his throat he asks me how Al Yatun is 'these days'. 'Busy,' is my reply. Commandant Evans has a fearsome reputation within the Battalion. As the Battalion Executive Officer he is responsible for all military discipline throughout the deployment. He also plays a pivotal role in assessing the performance of all junior officers – such as myself. I am quite frankly expecting a bollocking of some sort.

Instead, Commandant Evans leans forward and, in a conspiratorial tone, mock whispers, 'Us Dubs have to stick together? Right?' As I nod dumbly, he informs me that he has selected me to lead the 'Holy Land Tour' to Israel. In other words, a seventy-two-hour pass out of the Irish Area of Operations. Seventy-two hours out of uniform. Seventy-two hours in Israel. Three nights in Jerusalem. I can hardly believe my ears. The only snag is – and it turns out to be a major snag – that I will be the only officer on the trip with responsibility for the thirty or so troops on the 'organised' tour. 'And most of them,' according to Commandant Evans, 'are from A Company.' My blood runs cold.

The following Monday morning at 5 AM I marshal the twenty or so troops from A Company into the convoy of armoured personnel carriers as we head for Naqoura, the last UN position on the border between Lebanon and Israel. We pass through Qana and head for the coastal road between Tyre and Naqoura. I check the guys for flak jackets as we move through the olive groves and scented orange blossoms at the coast. The weather is unseasonably warm. I'm feeling optimistic. Then a voice from the dim interior of the APC, 'It's not flak jackets we need Sir, its fuckin' strait jackets.' There is a hearty chorus of cheers and much laughter. By now, I've learned to ignore the comedians.

We arrive in Naqoura – UNIFIL Headquarters on the Mediterranean coast. We check in our weapons with the Irish contingent. They will be held for us until our return on Thursday evening. We then change into civilian clothing. We have each brought one set of 'civvies' from Ireland. It is the first time in over two months I've been out of uniform. I catch sight of myself in the mirror. The jeans and shirt look familiar. My face however – sunburned and windburned as it is from constant patrolling – looks different. I think for a minute I have the appearance of someone who has been sleeping rough. Then I look at the lads. We look like a group of psychopaths. Mad Bastard is among the group. He gives me the thumbs up and shouts something unprintable about the 'wimmin in Jerusalem'. It's official. We are indeed an unsavoury bunch.

A couple of UN minibuses take us across the border to Ros Haniqra. The Israeli border defences are a labyrinth of concrete and steel structures. Covered in sensors, cameras, aerials and antennae. The Israeli troops are friendly. They welcome us to Israel. Young guys and girls. Younger than us, they look like secondary school kids on a transition year placement. There are a range of accents. The young officer in charge of the search area is from New York. He shakes hands with me and tells me that he plans to visit Dublin some day soon. 'As soon as my military service is up.' He has read Joyce and asks me to write down the names of some good 'literary bars' in Dublin. I scribble down the names of The Palace Bar on Fleet Street along with Kehoe's and McDaid's off Grafton Street. I tell him to read Flann O'Brien.

The troops are relaxed and are exchanging remarks with the young Israeli conscripts. 'Ye must be bored out of yer bleedin' mind,' remarks Sergeant Fuckin-Fuck. 'But don't worry, I'm sure there'll be another war comin' along any day soon.' There is a sudden awkward silence. Everyone, including the Israeli officer, bursts out laughing. He threatens to make us sing 'Molly Malone'. The lads threaten to sing 'Seven Drunken Nights'. One of the Israelis then gives us the opening line from 'Dirty Old Town'. He gets a round of applause. He is from the Ukraine. He tells us that his favourite band is the Pogues.

Eventually we exit on the Israeli side of the border. The difference between Lebanon and Israel – over a few hundred metres – is hard to comprehend. It is a complete culture shock. No more rutted tracks and ramshackle roadside shacks. Israel is California. The coastal road south is like Ventura Highway. We are introduced to our tour guide, Amin, who announces that ethnically, he is Druze. He also tells us over the PA of the tour bus that 'I drive tank with Golani Brigade of Israeli Army. And I see the Irish in 1982 when we pass through the Irish checkpoints during our invasion, north to Beirut. And I see the Irish soldiers drinking tea.' He gets an enthusiastic round of applause from the troops. This is obviously not the first time he's had the Irish on his bus.

Our first stop is Tiberias, which we reach mid morning. Amin brings the guys down to the shores of the Sea of Galilee to show them where Jesus walked on the water. A special treat for the lads. An open-air mass on the Mount of the Beatitudes. Blessed are the Peacemakers indeed. I slip away into the town. The main street of Tiberias is bathed in sunshine. Families are going about their business. The familiar streetscape makes me homesick. It is heartbreaking. I see a bank of public telephones. Up to now, I've been confined to a weekly telephone call to Ireland on the satellite phone in Irishbatt. I decide to ring my girlfriend. I go into the nearest shop to buy a phone card. The Israeli shopkeeper looks at me when he hears my accent.

'Who are you calling?' he asks.

'Ehh. My girlfriend.'

He tut tuts and blows air through his teeth. 'Not good my friend. I'll tell you what. Here's the deal. You use my phone in the office here. No charge. I won't take money from someone who wants to talk to his loved ones. You talk to your sweetheart. Tell her you love her. Ask her to marry you. Whatever. But, make sure you call your Mama. That's the deal. Talk to your mother. Then you can have as much time as you like. On me.'

He ushers me into his back office. Shows me how to get an international line to Ireland. I see the picture of his son on the wall. In IDF uniform. I call my girlfriend. The phone rings out. I call home. My Dad answers the phone. 'Good, I've been waiting to talk to you while your mother is out.' He tells me that my Mum is sick. 'It's cancer. It's called multiple myeloma.' The shopkeeper, Mr Fine, gives me some strong coffee. He tells me to come back 'any time' to use the phone. I tell him about my mother. He embraces me in that back room. The kindness of strangers.

We spend the first night in Jerusalem. In the Pilgrim's Palace Hotel in the Arab quarter, just opposite the Damascus Gate to the Old City. Sergeant Fuckin-Fuck and the lads head off to Jaffa Street and the Underground Nightclub. I walk the walls. Literally. The Walls of Jerusalem. Through Herod's Gate. Out the Dung Gate. I think of my mother. I walk along the Via Dolorosa. I manage a little laugh at the irony. A trader approaches me in the Souk and asks me if I'd like to see his 'beautiful' shop. I'm not in the mood for shopping. So, I try Sergeant Fuckin-Fuck's approach. 'Fuck Off.' He pursues me for three blocks – pointing me out to all and sundry. 'This infidel tells ME to fuckoff. I tell HIM to fuckoff.' I get a chorus of abuse for my trouble.

From there, I flee the Old City and head in any direction. My mind still reeling. I eventually come across the Israel Museum of Art. I'm staring at the building – Israel's largest cultural institution. I see it is open until 9 PM. A security guard is smoking and eyes me curiously. He asks me if I am a soldier. 'Its free in for soldiers,' he tells me. Inside I find a brochure containing images of Avner Ben-Gal's paintings. His exhibition, Avivit, has taken place earlier in the museum. I note he is born on exactly the same day as myself. Two very different lives. Two very different sets of experience. But, common ground nonetheless. His ghostly, haunting images speak directly to me of Lebanon. The raw emotion and desolation captured in his brush strokes calm me down. Pull me in like a centrifuge. So, now I can think straight. I can move back out into the street and breathe again. I no longer feel frantic. No longer feel the desire to tell everyone to fuck off. Another stranger in a strange place has spoken to me. Directly.

I eventually find myself in the Arizone Bar in downtown Jerusalem. Chatting to Israelis. Watching the Israeli girls dancing. Some in uniform. Dancing around their automatic rifles which they lay on the floor. In the same way some girls in Dublin dance around their handbags.

The next day we visit the Yad Vashem Holocaust Memorial. We enter a subterranean chamber in complete darkness. The light slowly increases. There is a mountain of shoes in the centre of the room. Children's shoes. The shoes of Jewish children sent to the gas chambers. The museum follows the relentless timeline of the Holocaust. Black and white photos of entire Jewish family groups appear on the walls. Photographed at happy family occasions in cities throughout Europe in the 1920s and 30s. Their silent faces smiling at the camera. Beautiful boys and girls. Babies. Proud parents. Unaware that they were about to be singled out. Selected and systematically murdered. For being Jewish. For no other reason. The family photographs catch me off guard and whisper the truth of the Holocaust. Much more so than the detailed descriptions of the death camps or the graphic photographs of the dead. The photos put names and faces to the victims. Pictured in the elegant salons and humble living rooms of European cities, the photos are also an explicit and clear communication of place. They firmly locate their murders – and murderers – within Europe. The cradle of modernity and modernism.

I'm told that Yad means 'place'. Vashem means 'name'. For me, Yad Vashem names the countless unknown dead. It reclaims the memory of those millions of unknown Jewish boys and girls murdered in Europe. Yad Vashem recalls those families with no resting place. In short, Yad Vashem is the precise opposite of 'unknown'. It makes the unknown knowable, speaks the unspeakable.

Then I think about the Katyusha missiles that I have seen fired into Israel by Hizbullah. In military-speak, fired at 'Destination Uniform Kilo' – or destination unknown. This phrase has been playing on my mind. Troubling me. Uniform Kilo. Un Known. The military euphemism for an indiscriminate, point blank attack seems to communicate the opposite of Yad Vashem. As though the term 'Unknown' renders the attack somehow neutral, impersonal. When in fact the opposite is the case. And in that moment I realise the significance of Hizbullah's indiscriminate missile attacks on Israel. Hizbullah mean to kill. Any time. Any place. Any name. Any Israeli. Not a military strategy. Just blind hatred. Terrorism. I force myself to think about the Israeli villages and towns along the border with Lebanon. And I force myself to think of the Israeli children sleeping there. From Kiryat Shmona down to Netanya. Not just the Lebanese kids whom I see every day, but the Israeli kids also. The Israeli kids that are just beyond view, out of sight over the wadis and ridgelines of Lebanon. Just like the kids in the photos in Jerusalem. I think about the words Yad Vashem and their meaning.

I try to reconcile this thought with my role in Lebanon. I am thinking of Khalil Gibran, the Lebanese poet, and his words, 'Pity the Nation'.

Me aged eighteen months, 1968 –
early military ambitions?

*Left*: Garda Joseph Clonan, my grandfather,
1926, Dublin Metropolitan Region (DMR)
*Bottom left*: Garda Eugene Clonan, my father,
1956, Dublin Metropolitan Region (DMR)
*Below*: Lieutenant Tom Clonan, day of medal
parade, Al Yatun, South Lebanon (March 1996)

A family tradition: Lieutenant Tom Clonan, my father, Garda (Retired) Eugene Clonan and my brother, Lieutenant (Navy) Eugene Clonan (August 1996)

On manoeuvres in Glen of Imaal, Me (top left) with Cadet Ray Kenny, Cadet Rossa Coleman, Cadet Paul Clarke and Cadet David Denieffe, all members of the 66th Cadet Class

Bicycles on parade, 66th Cadet Class on the square of Pearse Barracks, Curragh Camp (January 1990)

On Blue Line, the border with Israel and Lebanon, shortly after Israeli withdrawal from Lebanon (2000)

Up in the back hatch of the SISU on day patrol, Shaqra, South Lebanon (October 1995)

An Israeli hilltop position and firebase, Irishbatt, South Lebanon (December 1995). There were several such firebases on the high ground throughout Irishbatt

Welcome to Al Yatun: five-star bomb-proof accommodation, courtesy of the Irish Army

Entrance: note the sandbags and wired gabions to protect from shrapnel and blast effects of artillery

UNIFIL Force Commander Lieutenant General Wozniac (Poland) pins my UNIFIL medal and UN Nobel Peacekeepers Medal to my lapel in Camp Shamrock, Tibnine, South Lebanon (March 1996)

Hands across the border: me shaking hands with an Israeli soldier through the barbed wire at Blue Line, the Lebanon-Israel border (2000)

Civilian refugees in Al Yatun, South Lebanon minutes before the shelling of Qana on 18 April 1996

UN position at Qana, South Lebanon, in flames, minutes after being hit by
Israeli artillery (18 April 1996)

As above, UN position at Qana in flames in the immediate
aftermath of Israeli shelling (18 April 1996)

Parents and relatives sit in shock amongst the dead at Qana, South Lebanon
(18 April 1996)

A Fijian UN soldier washes the bodies of children in order to assist in
identification, Qana, South Lebanon (18 April 1996)

And I pity the ordinary people of both Lebanon and Israel, for the injustices perpetrated on them by Hizbullah on the one hand, and Israeli political 'hard men' on the other.

We visit Nazareth and Bethlehem. Returning to Jerusalem we pass through an area of desert. In the growing darkness Amin draws my attention to Bedouin tents in the distance. There are colour televisions flickering inside their tents. Just visible from the road.

On that last night in Jerusalem myself and Sergeant Fuckin-Fuck gate crash a wedding in the Mount Zion Hotel. He asks me to call him John. We are invited to join in the dancing. 'John' is relentlessly pursued by an older lady related to the groom. He ends up – somehow – at the top table. Eating bread out of the bride's breadbasket. Telling her how she reminds him of his daughter in Dublin. He shows her a photograph of his daughter and boasts that she will be the first in his family to go to university. He explains that his overseas allowances will pay for her to study physiotherapy in Trinity College. He tells her – with real tears in his eyes – how beautiful she is. Thankfully, he does not use the F word.

Twelve hours later we are back in Naqoura. Back in uniform. Everyone is subdued. As our convoy heads back to the Hills, I watch the Star of David fluttering and receding on the rampart of the Ros Haniqrah checkpoint. The Israelis are no longer 'them'. 'They,' like the shopkeeper Mr Fine in Tiberias, have names and faces and families. They are not unlike the Lebanese that I have come to know.

# Chapter 16

# Only Ten Shopping Days to Christmas

*Leprechauns is bastards*

The night after our return to Irishbatt, I'm back on patrol near the village of Shaqra. It is after midnight and the moonlit village is asleep. Not a soul to be seen. We pass slowly through the narrow main street. I look up at the wooden shuttered windows on the upper floors of the old buildings. You could be in France. The architecture is similar. The French influence in Lebanon is very visible. From hand-lettered street signs in Arabic and French, to the viticulture and olive groves in the terraced fields stretching from Tyre all the way north to the Bekaa Valley. I'm musing on this when at 1.18 AM precisely an attack is launched at DFF 30 directly in front of us.

Hizbullah are firing 60mm mortars and heavy machine gun fire directly at the compound. They are firing from the wadi just below us to the left-hand side of the road. DFF 30 retaliates immediately. The road around us is being raked with heavy machine gun fire and I hear the thump thump thump of counter mortar fire coming from the compound. Stones and pebbles are being thrown up all around us. The Sisu lurches to a halt and I hear the gearbox grinding below me as the Cavalry driver tries to get it into reverse. I realise he is trying to attempt a three point turn in the middle of the track. To turn around and get back to the cover of the village. But this will place us broadsides in the road in the middle of a shit storm. I put my hand over the throat microphone around my neck and say as clearly and as calmly as I can. 'Get out of the ditch. Get her back into gear. And get up that fucking track towards position 6-28. NOW please.'

I figure that the A Company observation post, 6-28 will give us some cover from the incoming rounds that are impacting all over the road. I see part of the tarmac in front of us rip open. Furrowed by point-five rounds. Miraculously, nothing hits us. The firing is above us and all around us. Somehow we escape injury. We come to a halt at the perimeter of 6-28. I can hear the infantry observers inside calling the shots from the compound over the battalion net. The duty officer comes over the Motorola. 'Avoid Alpha Route, over.' Too late for us. Corporal Burke, meanwhile, is on the edge. He is staring at me intently and his face has drained of colour. 'Jesus now. Oh, sweet Jesus,' is all he can manage.

The driver's voice crackles into my headphones. 'Only because you said please.' The firing from both sides continues for a further thirty minutes. DFF 30 adjusts its fire north towards A Company's other position at 6-28A, or Fraggle Rock as it is known by the troops. Directly below DFF 30's ramparts, the lads in Fraggle Rock are hammered for twenty minutes or so. They fire red flares. DFF 30 lifts and shifts its fire deeper into the Wadi. Hizbullah disappear.

When everything has died down, we chat to the A Company guys through the fence. They bring out a kettle. We drink tea with them. They give me letters to bring back to the A Company post room in Al Yatun. 'Can ye get our Christmas cards out for us?'

We head back down the track towards Shaqra. I signal our intention to return to Al Yatun to the duty officer in Camp Shamrock. 'Hello Zero. This is 41 Alpha. Mobile for Six Dash Four Zero. Out.' On the outskirts of Shaqra a powerful searchlight illuminates the lead Sisu. 'What now?' asks the driver. I twist around in the rear hatch and see that a searchlight on the perimeter of DFF 30 is trained on the lead Sisu. There is some activity on the perimeter fence. I'm wondering if they are going to fire on us. I make a decision there and then. I turn to Corporal Burke. 'Get the 84mm anti-tank gun up please.' I've decided that if they are going to fire at us, we might as well get one anti-tank round off at them. Fuck them. I wont go down without a fight. Corporal Burke's jaw drops. He stares at me open-mouthed. 'Ye what?' The driver has heard my request over his head-phones and he hits the accelerator. We tear through Shaqra and DFF 30 disappears from view. Luckily for all of us, Corporal Burke is still fiddling with the 84mm anti-tank gun as we pass through Tibnine. 'You can put that down now,' I tell him. His hands are shaking. But then, so are mine.

Nevertheless, I'm worried about Corporal Burke. I discuss his mental state with BS Begley and Sergeant Bracken back in Al Yatun. We resolve to keep an eye on him for the moment. For despite all of the wisecracking and the give and take between myself and the troops, everyone follows orders. I've never seen any of the troops, even the youngest guys and first-timers, hesitate to follow an order when the shit has hit the fan. This makes Corporal Burke's performance all the more worrying.

Meanwhile, December is a little quieter than the previous month. Hizbullah's attacks on the compounds have slowed down to one every four days on average. On 10 December they attack DFF 17, overlooking Haddathah. The attack and subsequent counterattack rages on for a few hours. The walls in Al Yatun shake and shudder with every salvo of artillery fired from Gate 12. Psycho announces 'Attention all personnel –

Remember, Only ten shoppin' days to Christmas.' We decorate the Communications Centre and Ops room with tinsel and fairy lights. Psycho now looks like an evil assistant in some alternative, gothic Santa's grotto.

An order from Battalion Headquarters informs us that in order to 'maintain morale' a large quantity of white paint has been made available to all units. We are advised to re-paint all 'exterior walls' and 'decorative stonework' before Christmas day. Funnily enough, the troops do not see this task as a 'morale booster' and complain bitterly at what they call 'dirty details'. Corporal Burke, though, takes to the task with gusto. He takes an inordinate amount of pleasure in hounding the young Troopers and Gunners from their rest periods and organising them into painting details. This leads to some competition – and friction – with A Company.

On one of my off days, I'm wandering past the billets where I encounter Sergeant Fuckin-Fuck harassing a group of infantry privates from A Company. They are dislodging the rocks at the edge of the path-ways and painting them white. 'Fer Christmas,' asserts the Sergeant.

I stand for a while watching proceedings. Sergeant Fuckin-Fuck eyes me suspiciously. Eventually I decide to say something officer-like.

'Shouldn't those men be wearing gloves?' I ask.

'Why?' retorts Sergeant Fuckin-Fuck somewhat defiantly; his usual tone of defiance, which is a carefully measured millimetre just short of insubordination. I ignore his habitual defiance and continue in my officer-pattern interrogation. I'm enjoying myself now.

'Because, those stones are the natural habitat of scorpions. It is likely that some will have taken shelter on the underside for the winter. If disturbed, they are likely to strike. Their venom is quite toxic to humans.' Sergeant Fuckin-Fuck glares at me.

'All right. Yis heard the fuckin' officer. There's a scorpion under one of them rocks. Whose urine is stingy to human beins. So. Go get your fuckin' gloves on. NOW!' he roars. 'Happy now, Sir?' he asks me.

I go to complete the weekly ordnance check with BS Begley. As usual, the BS has all of the weapons, ammunition, radios and ancillary equipment sorted and accounted for. He makes my job easy. As I initial the ordnance ledger and fill out the report forms, he tells me that we may need to deal decisively with Corporal Burke. 'He's shrink-wrapped. We might recommend some leave at Christmas. He needs some time out.' The constant shelling and firing have been playing on Corporal Burke's nerves. The BS continues, 'He's tormenting the lads with painting details. It would be good if it came from you.' I promise to ask him to lay off the troops.

I call into his billet with BS Begley. There is a full-scale row underway. Corporal Burke is backed into a corner with something tucked under his arm. Corporal Kennedy is advancing on him menacingly. We have arrived in the nick of time. 'What's going on lads?' enquires the BS gently. The BS interposes himself between the two corporals. His sheer physical size immediately defuses the situation. Corporal Kennedy appeals to me. 'We just want to put up a name on the billet. That's all. Like, put our stamp on it. After all that fuckin' painting.' He glares at Corporal Burke. Now it's his turn.

'It's a disgrace. Look at what they wanted to put up.' He shows me the wooden sign – presumably acquired from Hafif the Thief. It reads 'Rancho Relaxo'. I deem the sign inoffensive and Corporal Kennedy screws it to the door of the billet triumphantly.

Corporal Burke mutters darkly, 'Ye haven't fuckin' heard the last of this.'

That night I'm in the officer's mess, trying in vain to write a recommendation for a repatriation on humanitarian grounds for Corporal

Burke, when there is a commotion at the Communications Centre. Psycho activates the PA. 'Medical NCO to report to Communications Centre immediately.' I rush outside to find a delegation of Troopers and Gunners from the BMR gathered around Corporal Burke. His hands are cupped around his nose. There is blood on his hands and chin. 'What's happened?' I demand.

'Show him Burkey – show him, boy.' There is an unhealthy air of levity on the part of the troops. Corporal Burke lowers his hands. There is a dart – from the dartboard in the Canteen – stuck right through his nose. From left to right. Clean through the nostrils and septum. Not good. He's had a double nose piercing. He is clutching the dart tenderly. The troops are full of advice but light on sympathy. 'Pull the fuckin' thing out Burkey.' Corporal Burke gives a muffled reply.

'I can't do that. It'll do more damage on the way out.'

'Yeah, like one of them Indian arrows in the movies,' is the helpful reply. Corporal Burke looks at me plaintively.

'How did this happen?' I ask.

He replies mechanically, 'I walked out in front of the dartboard by accident.' The medics arrive and Corporal Burke is driven down to the Medical Aid Post in Shamrock. I later learn that the dart has been successfully removed by the medical officer. I'm told that his injuries are 'not life threatening'.

In the interim, I arrange for Corporal Burke to go home to Ireland for Christmas. We later have this extended to a permanent repatriation to Ireland on humanitarian grounds.

A few days later, RTÉ arrive in the Area of Operations. Treasa Davison has come to pre-record material for a Christmas broadcast for Ireland. The RTÉ crew stay in Camp Shamrock. They visit Al Yatun briefly where we corral them in the officer's mess for as long as possible.

The troops are lurking around. Sergeant Fuckin-Fuck wants to know if she'll 'play a fuckin' request'.

The inter-contingent soccer competition is also reaching its climax. Irishbatt and Ghanbatt are in the final. At the play-offs earlier in the tournament – played sporadically between attacks on the compounds – Ireland had been beaten by Ghanbatt in November. At the start of that match, one of the Ghanaian troops – an animist – had performed a powerful spiritual ritual on the pitch. An elaborate chanting and dance which led him up to the Irish goal. He leaped around the posts and threw handfuls of dirt and dust into the goal mouth. The Ghanaians were cheering wildly and we were more than a bit intimidated. Spooked. And the magic worked. Irishbatt got hammered three–nil.

So the final is a grudge match between the Irish and the Ghanaians. This time, the Ghanaian spiritual ritual is bolder, more elaborate. The Ghanaians are chanting and clapping. In total there are about 100 Irish and Ghanaian troops around the 'pitch'. When the display ends there is an unexpected development. Sergeant Fuckin-Fuck appears at the sideline in a full leprechaun outfit. There are wild cheers from the Irish. A deafening roar from the sideline as the 'leprechaun' dances a jig in the middle of the pitch and then sprints up to the Ghanaian goal. There, Sergeant Fuckin-Fuck throws a fistful of dirt across the line. That's when the pitch invasion starts. A half-dozen Ghanaians pursue the 'leprechaun' across the pitch and through the Irish spectators. Sergeant Fuckin-Fuck clambers up the side of the Sisu with surprising agility. With relief, I hear the clang of the top-hatch as he locks it from inside. Safe.

The match proceeds and – despite the provocation – is a stylish affair which goes to the wire. Ireland eventually win two–one. As we pass through the Ghanaian checkpoints, 'Hakuna Matata' is replaced with the cry 'Leprechauns is bastards'.

There is a lull in the fighting in the third week of December. On the 18th – a week before Christmas – a small convoy of Israeli vehicles emerges from Saff al Hawa and moves towards At Tiri at the edge of B Company. The BMR is put on alert and we roll out of Al Yatun and down the road to Haddathah. By this time, the Israelis have already withdrawn but they have left something in the roadway. Moving forward to investigate we find six Christmas trees. A gift to the Irish from the IDF. Corporal Kennedy suggests we give them to the Muktar. BS Begley patiently informs him that the Shia Muslims in Al Yatun don't celebrate Christmas. We put one of the trees up in Al Yatun. Even the old sweats and most hardened of the troops from A Company and the BMR agree that it is 'bleedin' great'.

Corporal Kennedy asks me if it is true that I was a 'bleedin' teacher'. I reply in the affirmative. He tells me he is studying for the Army's General Certificate of Education – the equivalent of the Junior Cert. I'm wondering if he is pulling my leg. Then the BS tells me that Corporal Kennedy is studying every night he is not on patrol. 'He's going to do his Leaving Cert too. When we get home.' Corporal Kennedy grins at me. For the next couple of weeks I help him with *Animal Farm*. 'Them pigs remind me of somethin',' he tells me. 'With them bein' more equal than others and all that. And havin' better food and clothes than the other animals. Like the bleedin' officers in this kip if ye ask me.' Corporal Kennedy, it seems, has acquired a firm grasp of Orwell's commentary.

# Chapter 17

# Christmas in the Holy Land

*A breakfast to remember*

On Christmas Eve, I join the queue of troops for the satellite phone. By some minor miracle my Mum answers the phone during the three minutes allotted to me. I'm looking anxiously around me and tell her in a whisper that I love her. With sixty seconds left I call my girlfriend. Miracle of miracles – she answers the phone on the second ring. 'Happy Christmas!' I blurt out. Then, throwing caution to the wind, 'And, eh, I love you.' She answers in a sleepy voice – which sounds very far away – 'And I love you too. Happy Christmas.' My heart is racing. Psycho is banging the door shouting 'Next.'

I emerge from the cubicle and Corporal Kennedy is standing there grinning at me. 'How many birds were you talkin' to there. I heard you tellin' two birds that you loved them.' I am trying to explain when the troops in the queue break out into an unhealthy round of applause and wolf whistles. Corporal Kennedy is extremely pleased with the result and punches me on the shoulder. 'Ye foxy fucker ye.' There is a loud cheer as I head back to my lonely billet.

I'm elated by my girlfriend's simple reply in our brief telephone call. However, in the loneliness of my billet that Christmas Eve, I am visited by the ghost of Christmas past. I think of my mother and father. I think of previous Christmases at home in Dublin. I remember our Christmas trees when I was a small boy, during the closing years of the 1960s. The wonder of tinsel and glass baubles on an artificial tree in the living room. Next to the curtains. I remember my mother swinging me around the kitchen with the Ronettes belting out 'Sleigh Ride' on the radio. I clearly remember the clip-clopping of hooves on that record and the firm belief that reindeer were on the roof of our terraced house in Finglas – a long way from the Arctic tundra. I remember in particular that starlit Christmas night in 1969 when my father stole into my bedroom with a present. He had just come off duty. 'Lates', as he called them. As he slipped into the room I woke up and sat bolt upright. Frozen in mid-step – and in full uniform – he whispered urgently, 'Go back to sleep, Santa's downstairs – the Gardaí are helping him this year.' My father was quick on his feet all right.

Many years later and I cannot sleep on this Christmas Eve either. Memories of my parents and my childhood come flooding over me. They are happy memories. A kaleidoscope of sunny summer days in our back garden on Ballygall Avenue. Under the apple trees. Playing in the rockery or in the conservatory. Poking sticks through gaps in my father's work-shop door where, miraculously, hens were kept. At first, my father had acquired a bantam cock from a trader on Moore Street. A city boy from Drumcondra, he was puzzled when the cock refused to lay eggs. But he was very impressed as it strutted over the ridge tiles of our terraced houses screeching out its cock-a-doodle-doo each morning at 5 AM. Our neighbours were less impressed. Mr O'Brien – our cheerful next-door neighbour – offered to kill 'that fucking duck' with a shovel. Eventually we got hens that laid eggs.

My Mum was Blaithin – little flower. She sometimes called me *An*

*Gamhain Breac* – the speckled calf. I was much loved. When I was four, I found a dead bird in the garden. Still warm. Its head and beak hanging curiously limp. I ran into the house and found my Mum folding sheets in the kitchen. In blinding sunlight. A halo of cotton fibres, twisting silver, shining in the air around her. She helped me to carefully place the bird into a cardboard box. We placed tissues around it, for its final nesting place. Blaithin helped me place the box – very gently – into a small hole we'd dug in the flower bed. 'Will you die?' I asked her. She reached down and pulled me to her. 'Of course not, my love.' I realise this Christmas night, in Lebanon, that of course she will die. I am beginning to realise that everything, everyone, dies in the end. Eventually, I slept.

Christmas Day in Al Yatun 1995 is a Christmas I will never, ever forget. As it happens, I'm not on duty. Not on patrol. The morning is frosty. The sky clear blue. The cooks have promised a breakfast to remember. I wander into the cookhouse where Pops the cook is ladling scrambled eggs and sausages onto plates. He is covered in sweat and his face is lit up like the Christmas tree on the roof of the canteen. There is an electric atmosphere in the cookhouse. Even the cockroaches seem more animated than usual. Then I notice the two wheelie bins at the end of the counter. They are brimming with a dark coloured liquid atop which is floating orange and lemon segments studded with cloves. There is a very strong smell of alcohol wafting off the warm, steaming liquid. Pops notices my gaze and rushes around the bain maries and hotplates to intercept me. He shoos some cockroaches off the bins and closes the lid.

'See?' he cries proudly. Beaming at me. And now I realise he is lit up with drink. 'I've thought of everything. Them cockroaches cant get into the gargle there with the lids closed. And don't worry about the hygiene either. I've lined these fuckers with black plastic bin-sacks.' I am gobsmacked.

'Eh, What gargle is this now?' I enquire.

The troops are dipping mugs, cereal bowls – anything they can lay there hands on – into the mysterious brew. 'This,' announces Pops proudly, 'is a hot fruit punch. For the lads on Christmas mornin' on account of it bein' cold and all.' I find out later that under some arcane UN Field regulation, that Al Yatun has been receiving a daily 'ration' of red wine since the beginning of our deployment. The aforementioned 'wine' is of a very rough variety indeed – from God knows where – and is stored in plastic drums. Pops has mixed it with what is anyone's guess to produce several wheelie bins full of hooch.

I'm still taking this in when Pops produces a mess tin with around half a pint of the stuff sloshing around in it. 'Go on Lieutenant Cloonan. Have a taste of it.'

'Ehh, that's Clonan,' I reply and take a mouthful. Fire and cinnamon are the first impressions. It burns its way down into my belly and I have to admit it tastes not too bad at all. It tastes of Christmas. The assembled troops shout their approval and take my lead as the green light to get stuck into the punch. It is 7 AM. I pull myself up and call out to Pops over the throng. Even though these are A Company troops, I feel I ought to voice my concerns over the liquid breakfast. 'Ehhh, Pops, is this wise?'

'Don't worry Lieutenant Cloonan,' he replies. 'We've another eight wheelie bins where that came from.'

Khalid Hakim welcomes me into the officer's mess for breakfast. We have bacon from Ireland which Mac had brought with him back in October. Frozen since then, it is a reminder of home. After that, we travel down to Camp Shamrock to attend the Operations Brief. The entire area of operations is quiet as the grave. Hizbullah are nowhere to be seen. Even the compounds are quiet. No activity on the perimeters. No patrols. No reconnaissance by fire. Not a sausage. The Battalion Executive Officer shakes hands with me and wishes me a Happy Christmas. He is pleased at the outcome of the Holy Land Tour. 'Well done Thomas. No one got arrested. That's unusual. I'll be detailing you to bring the Pipers to Damascus for the Saint Patrick's Day Parade in March.' Everyone laughs. I'm not sure why. But, I am pleased at the prospect of seeing Syria in the New Year.

We get back to Al Yatun in time for dinner. There are approximately a hundred troops crammed into the cookhouse. Into wheelie bin six at this point. The officers traditionally serve dinner on Christmas day. Pops announces our arrival by banging a large saucepan with a metal ladle. The lads give us a loud boozy welcome and we work our way up and down the tables handing out plates of turkey and spuds. Everyone is in good spirits with the exception of the thirty or so guys who are on duty and standby that day. They watch – in sober detachment – as the festivities reign.

Pops and the senior NCOs usher the officers out of the cookhouse. As the late afternoon turns to darkness, I wander up to the back observation post. I climb the tower and sit with Sergeant Bracken, who is on duty inside the OP. We drink coffee and stare at the intense red sky and sunset over Lebanon. Sergeant Bracken has three small children at home. He looks at his watch. 'They'll be in bed by now. They got bicycles this year. A note from Daddy on them. I wrote the notes in August. Imagine.'

I walk through the darkness back to the officer's mess. There is loud singing and quite a ruckus from the dining hall. Pops has been in there since 5 AM. Every few minutes there is a deafening roar of approval and cheers from inside the cookhouse. I wonder what in the name of God the lads are up to. I'm sorely tempted to go in and investigate. But Sergeant Bracken has warned me not to go in there – no matter what. I pass by the Communications Centre. Psycho has taken the day off. A duty signaler is monitoring the radios. He looks up. 'Dead as a fuckin' doornail.' Khalid tells me that for dinner there is 'Turkey and white thing with green thing.' Myself, Mac and the officers from A Company eat our dinner. We drink Kafraya. We squeeze into our small bar and drink to our families and loved ones. We play the Elvis Presley CD again. And then we play the Cole Porter songs.

At around 8 PM, the troops abandon the cookhouse for the canteen. We watch from the roof of the officers mess as Mad Bastard leads a conga line of A Company soldiers the short distance to the canner. The gunners manning the machine gun post over the checkpoint watch wistfully from above. 'He'll have a fuckin' sore head tomorrow, so he will.'

Around midnight, I return to my own billet. Climb in under the mosquito net. I think of everyone at home in Ireland. Then, I sleep like the dead.

St Stephen's day brings sore heads to all and sundry in Al Yatun. Mercifully, however, it is quiet once again throughout the AO. The Padre comes calling. He brings hummus and tabouli from the local Muktar along with fresh baked flat bread from the women in the village. Later, he says mass in the cookhouse. The wheelie bins are nowhere to be seen.

The following morning, on 27 December, Hizbullah attack DFF 17 at Haddathah in a dawn assault. The Israelis retaliate and there is mayhem throughout Irishbatt. The neighbouring Israeli compounds open fire simultaneously in the pre-dawn gloom. Interlocking arcs of fire between the firebases ensure that the entire AO is caught up in the retaliatory fire. The Israeli artillery positions at Gate 12 and Gate 14 Alpha soon join in. I listen to the radio traffic in the Sisu. Ready to move out when the fighting eases. Ready to recover the dead or injured. There is sporadic fire all that day and night. The Israeli artillery bracket their fire around Al Yatun and shrapnel from the 155 shells whines and smacks around the post. The Christmas tree is hit. It sags and eventually slides off the roof of the canteen.

On the following morning, the Israeli compound at DFF 17, overlooking Haddathah is assaulted again. This time, Hizbullah manage to manoeuvre right up to the perimeter fence and look like they might even breach the defences. I'm lying flat on the roof, watching the firefight through binoculars. The Israelis are throwing grenades over the perimeter wall and directing small arms fire at Hizbullah. Still, they press their attack. The firefight reaches a crescendo. Then silence. Psycho's voice below over the PA. 'Bodies in the wadis. Stand by.'

On the following day, 29 December, Hizbullah infiltrate as far south as Saff al Hawa and Bint Jubayl. They assault DFF 24 in an attack that commences at last light and continues until midnight. The next day, Hizbullah fire Katyusha missiles into Israel from Tibnine. The Observation Post at 6-48 log the attack. 'Armed Elements firing Katyusha rockets. Destination Uniform Kilo.' The Duty Operations officer records the attack into Israeli territory. 'Twelve missiles from 1 Km NE of Post 6-43 to unknown location.'

On the following morning – Saturday, 30 December – the Israelis step up their activity within Irishbatt's area of operations. We note a substantial increase in activity from within the firebases. At around 3 PM, an IDF tracked command vehicle is seen approaching DFF 23 or Brashit Compound. Presumably with reinforcements. Perhaps with some IDF officer on board charged with bringing things under control. Five minutes later, Hizbullah fire a Sagger missile from the ridgeline just north of Al Yatun. It hits the tracked vehicle. We see a puff of smoke as the missile strikes it. Then seconds later a loud metallic clang reverberates around the wadis. The missile does not seem to have exploded – but the kinetic energy of the round has driven it straight through the Israeli armour. The firebases erupt once more and the entire area is raked with artillery, mortar and tank fire. Irishbatt goes into Groundhog. At 3.30 or so, the firebases suddenly fall silent. A swarm of Israeli helicopters swoop low over the opposite ridgeline. As they loop the wadis and provide aerial cover, two Israeli casualties are medically evacuated by a chopper bearing red crosses. Hizbullah continues to pour small arms fire in that general direction.

# Chapter 18

# Happy New Year

*78 Irishbatt Operations Summary January 1996*
*Shooting Incidents: 139, Firings Close to Irishbatt Positions:11, Serious Incidents*
*involving armed elements:19, Air Incursions by Israeli Aircraft: 2*
Unit History, 78 Irishbatt, UNIFIL

New Year's Eve in Lebanon is relatively uneventful. After the fighting of the previous few days, Sunday, 31 December is quiet. Mac informs me that the Muktar Rafiq Haydar Hazimi has invited the officers of Al Yatun to dinner in his villa that afternoon.

At around three in the afternoon, we take our flak jackets and helmets and travel as passengers in a Sisu to be deposited outside the Muktar's villa at the edge of Haris. It feels strange to be squatting in the belly of the Sisu, as opposed to standing up in the hatch, wired into the radio nets. It feels claustrophobic in the dark interior as the Sisu roars, bumps and crashes down into the village. I think of the Israelis in the APC yesterday. It doesn't pay to think too much about their injuries.

We climb out of the APC and are greeted by the Muktar and his entourage of sullen bearded bodyguards. They escort us through the gates of the villa. We have left our rifles in the vehicle and are only carrying sidearms – Browning automatic pistols. Motorola radios are shoved deep into our combat uniforms on silent mode. The villa is an ancient, rambling building. Red-tiled roof, climbing plants everywhere. On the outside of the villa, the render is unpainted and crumbling in places. But on the inside its décor and furnishings are exquisite. We enter a large reception hall and remove our flak jackets. I take in our surroundings. The white marble floor is gleaming. On the walls, there are tiles with Byzantine patterns. Heavy cushions and drapes everywhere.

We are ushered into a large dining room and invited to sit on cushions around a low table. We wash our hands at bowls of water at each place setting, drying them in the starched white cloths provided.

The Muktar then claps his hands and the female members of his household enter carrying large platters of food. The Muktar – remembering me from our fraught introduction – has me seated at his right-hand side. He motions a young woman towards me. 'Please, for Lieutenant Cloonan – the beautiful birds please.' The girl flourishes the tray upon which sit row upon row of roasted songbirds. Finches, thrushes and all manner of exotic birdies. They lie there forlornly – anatomically complete with half-closed eyes and pitifully singed and scorched feathers.

The Muktar motions at me eagerly and urges me to eat. All eyes are on me as I have been accorded the privilege of the first taste of the meal. It would be an appalling display of bad manners to refuse or even hesitate. I am panicking ever so slightly and pick the smallest bird on the tray. I pick it up gently between my fingers. It is almost weightless. Determined not to offend, I pop the entire bird into my mouth and swallow it whole in one hard swallow. I feel the bird's claws and beak scraping along the back of my throat as it goes down. I suppress a vomit reflex and force a broad smile.

The Muktar and his entourage are very impressed and give me a small round of applause. Even the sullen bearded ones are looking at me with a new-found respect. For as I discover – while watching them eat – the time-honoured method for eating small birds is to delicately pull the breast-meat from the bone between forefinger and thumb. The feathers and the rest of the carcass – beak included – are then daintily discarded.

The Muktar professes amazement at my ability to eat the entire bird. 'Lieutenant Cloonan eat the whole bird. He is very strong man. For such a small man.' Mac is trying hard to control his laughter at the opposite side of the table. My fellow officers are enjoying my second meeting with the Muktar almost as much as the first.

That night, as midnight strikes, the entire area of operations lights up with gunfire. Again. The hilltop positions fire wildly in all directions as tracer rounds arc through the moonlit night. The villages below reverberate with gunshots and flares. Everyone, all sides, Israelis and Lebanese alike, celebrate the New Year by wildly firing whatever weapon they can lay their hands on. We are watching all of this from the roof of the officer's mess in Al Yatun. We toast the new year, 1996, with Almaza – the local Lebanese beer. All is well. We have reached the halfway point of our tour of duty in Lebanon. Spent and stray rounds however are pinging and whining around us. A point-five round hits the cistern block and drains Al Yatun of all of its water. Psycho announces immediate water rationing. We call it a day.

As I meander through the post, the diesel generators are thrumming their exhaust fumes across the billet blocks and blast wall defences. Sporadic gunfire echoes from the wadis below us. I think of Dublin and the countdown to New Year. They are two hours behind us in Al Yatun. As I go to sleep it is still 1995 in Ireland. The New Year will be rung in Christchurch as Al Yatun sleeps.

At 2 AM I wake to a loud screeching of metal and a sickening thud. I am certain that an artillery round has hit the post. But no explosion – yet. My mind is racing as I scramble into my desert boots, grab flak jacket, weapon and helmet and sprint for the Ops room. But Al Yatun is silent. No one else seems to have heard the sound. I stop running near the canteen and scan the billet blocks. No movement. No sign of impact. And there is no firing or shelling from the Israeli positions. Total silence. Nothing out of the ordinary except what looks like two searchlights pointing skyward from the rear of the post. I move cautiously in that direction and begin to hear whispered voices and hushed, urgent entreaties. 'Are ye all right, Smithy?' As I round the corner of the shower blocks, I see Sergeant Bracken standing next to a huddle of troops. Beyond them, in the newly dug septic tank, is a UN four-wheel-drive Jeep. It has been driven backwards into the septic tank pit. It is now resting on the rear bumper with its headlights pointing skyward.

The Cavalry fitters – who maintain the fleet of armoured vehicles in Al Yatun – are standing around sheepishly. Next to them stands Corporal Smith with a black eye and a rapidly swelling nose.

'What's going on lads?' I enquire. Sergeant Bracken – who is duty sergeant – informs me that Corporal Smith and the fitters have been victims of 'a case of misadventure'. They had been arguing over the gearbox in the four-wheel-drive Jeep. Something about the amount of torque. Corporal Smith had argued, it seems, that according to *What Car?* magazine, the gearbox on the Jeep could cope with the steep sides of 'even the steepest wadi'. They tested their theory out at 2 AM on the slope of the pit that the engineers had dug for the septic tank. Gravity won.

The following morning the UN vehicle is back in the vehicle park. It has been panel beaten, re-sprayed and restored to its original condition overnight. Corporal Smith's nose was not broken. But his ego was severely dented. No amount of panel beating would fix that. From now on, Corporal Manus Smith is known as Minus.

January proves to be a very busy month from an operational point of view. Hizbullah now carry out at least one attack every forty-eight hours. They concentrate their attacks on the Cuckoo's Nest or DFF 13 near Rshaf, along with Haddathah Compound (DFF 17) and Brashit Compound (DFF 23). The Israelis retaliate as a matter of course and there is an escalation of violence in Irishbatt's AO throughout January. It intensifies after the start of Ramadan on Monday, 22 January. The haunting Call to Prayer in the villages within Irishbatt's AO is more often than not accompanied by high velocity rifle fire and escalating gun battles between Hizbullah and the IDF. Hizbullah have ignored Ramadan and are pressing hard their attacks on the Israelis.

During the first week of January, I learn that my mother's condition does not warrant 'heroic' treatment measures. No bone marrow transplant. Her deteriorating condition is to be 'managed' instead. Chemo and radiotherapy. My Dad tells me on the phone – in his matter-of-fact way – that she will be wearing a wig when I get back to Ireland. I wonder about the implications of all of this.

On 7 January, Hizbullah launch their first attack of the year on the Cuckoo's Nest at DFF 13. My least favourite Israeli firebase is attacked at 4.07 AM. This kicks off a deteriorating cycle of attack, retaliation and counterattack. Throughout all of this, the BMR continues to patrol. Night and day. The patrols blur into an ongoing loop of increasingly frantic radio traffic. The AO repeatedly plunged into firefights and shellfire. No predictable pattern. The attacks occur at all times of the day and night. Sudden gunfire followed immediately by dozens of simultaneous shooting reports over the radio. The tinny hissing company and battalion nets flooded with coordinates, timings and weapon and calibre types. 'Hello Zero, 40 X medium mortar high explosive and 500 rounds heavy machine gun fire from DFF 23 to approximate map reference Haris, over.' Then the Motorola, clear and close-up, with the duty operations officer informing us 'Hello 41 Alpha. Be advised. Gate 12 is firing into your grid location over.'

Normally, we receive these 'newsflashes' as the rounds are falling around us. Or 'incoming', as it is called in the movies. At that point we are 'outgoing' – as fast as we can. But never knowing if we are fleeing into the bracketing, probing artillery – or away from it, to safety. It is nerve-racking. But nobody ever mentions that. For that is taboo. We talk about the awful weather, our girlfriends, what everyone is doing in Ireland. But we never, ever, talk about the fear and uncertainty. And we all know now – only too well – from collecting the bodies from the wadis, what the various weapons can do to the frail human body. Irrespective of flak jackets and helmets.

Night after night in that dark January we patrol the villages of Rshaf, Bayt Yahun, Shaqrah, Jumay Jumay, Majdal Silm. Names as familiar to me as Glasnevin, Phibsboro, Constitution Hill, the North Quays. I can still recite the names of these sleeping, moonlit villages with whom I became so intimately acquainted.

# Chapter 19

# Finnbatt Range

*Kuka vittu sinä olet? (Who The Fuck Are You?)*

On Monday, 8 January, I am summoned to Camp Shamrock to see the Battalion Executive Officer once more. I meet Commandant Evans in his office. He smiles as I enter and offers me a choice of tea or coffee. The omens are good. He pours me a coffee and invites me to sit. 'I've some good news and some bad news,' is his opener. The good news – apparently – is that the Battalion Commander has agreed to my appointment as officer in charge of the Pipe Band's trip to Damascus in March for the St Patrick's Day celebrations there. It is still news to me that St Patrick's Day is celebrated in Syria. But apparently so. I had suspected that this was a practical joke. So, I am delighted. We will be travelling through Israel and across the Israeli-Syrian border.

The bad news is that a French Colonel – based in UNIFIL Headquarters in Naqoura – has ordered that Irishbatt fire 12,000 rounds of ammunition on the range in Finnbatt. Apparently, 12,000 rounds of rifle ammunition is our training allotment for the tour of duty. And due to the constant fighting in the AO, we haven't had time to get each individual soldier within the battalion to the ranges to do practice shoots. We've been, to say the least, 'otherwise engaged.' However, according to

Commandant Evans, the French Colonel has 'a firm grasp of the non-essentials' and compares him to 'a lighthouse in the Bog of Allen. Brilliant, but useless'. He has insisted – irrespective of the operational conditions in Irishbatt – that we fire our training allotment. Period.

Commandant Evans sits back in his chair and exhales in frustration. He looks at me over the rim of his coffee cup and puts a proposal to me. 'Thomas, we don't have the capacity at the moment to stage multiple training shoots over in Finnbatt. The logistics alone . . .' He pauses. 'We were thinking, it might be useful if a select group from the BMR were to go to the range and, say, fire off the 12,000 rounds in a half a day?' The thoughts of firing 12,000 rounds, point blank into the wadi – did have a certain appeal to me. 'We'd have to write up the expenditure and that would keep our French friend happy. But, we need someone discreet. Someone mature – like yourself, Thomas – to keep it, in-house, shall we say.'

I duly agree and we proceed to the operations room. Commandant Evans has a spring in his step. We book the rifle range in Finnbatt for the following day. He then refers me to a Logs officer who signs out the 12,000 rounds of ammo. It takes us about an hour to load the boxes into the Sisu. As we fill up with diesel and roar out the gate, Commandant Evans salutes me from the central square of Camp Shamrock. He calls up to me, 'Don't forget Thomas – us Dubs need to stick together. Omerta, if you know what I mean.' He then makes a cutthroat gesture with his finger.

The next day, myself, Corporal Smith, Corporal Kennedy and Sergeant Bracken head down to Finnbatt – the Finnish Battalion area. The range as such is little more than an abandoned wadi with a cliff face at the rear – acting as a back stop for the rifle rounds. As we dismount however, we notice some changes at the range. Some new developments.

Somehow, an old Lebanese Army jeep has been abandoned where the targets are normally fixed. It presents a natural target. On close inspection – all the while cautious for booby traps and mines – I notice that the engine is missing. Someone has towed the jeep and left it in the target area. Not only that, someone has also built a small replica of an observation post, complete with concrete blocks and sandbag reinforcement. It looks like a tiny thatched cottage. Sergeant Bracken scratches his head and smiles at me. 'Well, at least we've something to fire our 12,000 rounds at!'

Like schoolboys, we race back to the firing point and begin eagerly unloading boxes of ammunition from the Sisu. A swarm of Lebanese kids arrive. Barefoot, skinny kids. Kids from the poorest Lebanese families, they always converge on the firing point to gather up the brass cartridges ejected during training shoots. It suits us. It keeps the firing point tidy and gives the kids something to trade with in the local towns and villages. A plastic shopping bag full of brass cartridges can fetch five dollars. A fortune for these little guys and girls. The troops also enjoy the kids' company and – as usual – give them all of their food, chocolate, cash. Often, the kids also get all of the ration packs in the vehicles. The kids remind the troops of home. I'm amazed at the effect these kids have on the troops. Otherwise hard men turn into grinning idiots around little Lebanese kids.

The usual drama unfolds on the firing point as Corporal Kennedy heads straight for the Sisu. 'That young one looks hungry, Sir. Just hold on a sec, I want to get him me sandwiches. I'm fat enough already.' Corporal Smith has been mugged by two ten year old boys who have already stolen his field dressing and a pack of probiotic yoghurts he had brought in his backpack. To reduce cholesterol apparently.

Sergeant Bracken is down on his hunkers handing out chocolate and cash to the kids. They are pitifully thin. Some of them are filthy. Hair matted, clothes torn. They look cold in the harsh sunshine. It is a frosty day and most of them are wearing just T-shirts. I notice four who look like siblings. They hang together at the rear of the group and are too shy to push forward for food and other booty. I flank around the throng and give the eldest kid, a boy of about eleven, my lunch, ration packs, field dressing and all the cash I have on me. Unlike the others, he does not run off crowing and screeching in triumph. Instead, he gathers his two brothers and little sister into a huddle. I watch him divide out the food, carefully and methodically. Everybody gets an equal share. He constantly looks back at me with his big brown eyes. Nervously. He is jumpy. Like a kid who has been beaten or abused in some way. He has a cold sore on his lip. His big eyes are watering with chronic conjunctivitis. I make a mental note to ask the medics in Shamrock to come down to the range and take a look at the kids.

His little sister is less shy. She smiles up at me through her curly hair and holds out her hand. Sergeant Bracken is laughing at me. 'You may forget about it, Sir – She's got you wrapped around her little finger.' The youngest boy is wearing a faded Muppet T-Shirt with a cheeky looking Kermit the Frog on the front. Kermit is waving hello. The oldest boy shepherds them off to the rear of the Sisu to eat their food.

Corporal Kennedy has prized open most of the boxes and we begin filling magazines from the foil cases of bullets. 5.56 mm French bullets. Fabrique en France. The word 'Explosiv' is stencilled on the side of the boxes over a skull and crossbones. Corporal Kennedy teases me about this. 'Here, Sir, you officers do your bleedin' Leavin Cert. What does 'Explosiv' mean?' Even Corporal Smith laughs. We are in high spirits. There are just the four of us. Corporal Smith runs up to the back-stop on the range and raises a red flag to indicate we are about to commence firing. Corporal Kennedy has wrapped a green scarf around his head making him look like Rambo as he raises the Steyr into the firing position. Aiming carefully he squeezes off the entire magazine on automatic. A loud buzz as the rounds shatter the glass on the Lebanese jeep. The Steyr barely registers any recoil. Stays on target. 'Fuckin magic!' shouts Corporal Kennedy. Sergeant Bracken and Corporal Smith open fire simultaneously on the mini thatch cottage. Masonry flies up in the air as they methodically destroy the structure. Sandbags burst and ricochets sing around the foot of the cliff. We all join in. Firing hundreds, thousands of rounds in minutes. The weapons become so overheated that we lay them down carefully and re-commence firing with other weapons.

Eventually the Jeep goes on fire. The noise of our firing is deafening. Corporal Kennedy has discarded his shirt and is firing from the hip – Rambo style. The kids are feverishly collecting the hot brasses. There is much cheering on the firing point and it takes all of my efforts to keep the kids back – to the rear of the shooters.

The jeep has now completely disintegrated and the thatch cottage has disappeared altogether. Some of the sand bags are smouldering. The patchy grass at the foot of the backstop has caught fire and is generating a great deal of smoke which is billowing out over the cliff face and into the wadi. 'War is hell!' screams Corporal Kennedy as he slaps another magazine into the Steyr.

I keep two ammunition boxes full of cartridge cases for the shy kids. I call out to them in Arabic. '*Kifak*.' They approach hesitantly, snatch the boxes and scamper away. The little girl calls out '*Shukran*.' The little boy in the Kermit T-Shirt calls out '*shaitan*' and throws an apple butt at me which catches me full in the face. Corporal Kennedy bursts out laughing. 'He fuckin' called you Satan. He has you sussed all right.'

Just then we see a cloud of dust along the roadway as two Finnbatt jeeps speed towards us. We squint into the sunshine to see who our visitors might be. The vehicles roar up and come to a screeching halt. 'Put on your fucking shirt,' snarls Sergeant Bracken at Corporal Kennedy as he clears his throat. 'Eh, Sir, I think these guys want to speak to you.'

A Finnish Major jumps out of the lead vehicle. He is clearly agitated. I smile winningly at him. '*Kuka vittu sinä olet?*' he asks me. Roughly translated, this means, 'Who the fuck are you?'

He then gestures at the range. It turns out that the Finnish Minister for Defence is visiting Finnbatt today. Of all days. And the Finns had industriously set up a variety of targets on the range in order to give the Finnish Minister and his VIP party a firepower demonstration. Gulp. We've wrecked Finnbatt Range. Major Patosalmi casts a cold eye over Corporal Kennedy who is grinning at him and notices my rank markings. Yet again he gestures at the range and asks me '*Miksi vitussa sinä niin teit?*' His Sergeant, who is clearly amused at this exchange between officers translates for me. 'The Major wants to know why you destroyed our targets?'

I gather my wits together and decide to front it as best I can. I take two steps toward him – a technique I've seen Corporal Kennedy use in heated arguments. He immediately steps back. An unexpected development. 'Is it within range standing orders to leave that sort of shit all over the target area?' I ask him as forcefully as I can. The Sergeant rapidly translates. The Major reddens and fires off a long staccato sentence in Finnish. Full of emphasis and pauses. But, he seems on the defensive now. A larger convoy of Finnish vehicles is now fast approaching. Sergeant Bracken whistles and observes 'Here's the Minister now, Sir. I think its best if you do the talking.'

The Finnish Minister and his entourage approach the firing point. The Finnish military personnel look very angry indeed. But, the Minister himself is delighted to meet some 'Irish soldiers.'

'I went to Trinity College in the 1972,' he tells me. I feel a surge of relief. I tell him I am also a graduate of TCD. It turns out we both studied Irish literature. He and I share an interest in Flann O'Brien of all people. I recite for him 'A Pint of Plain'. He finishes each line with me. He pumps my hand furiously and then grabs me in a bear hug. Major Patosalmi is mystified. On the way back to Irishbatt, Sergeant Bracken calls me 'Nine Lives'. I now have a proper nickname. However, our exploits on Finnbatt Range have been reported to the Operations Staff in Camp Shamrock. We are notorious it seems. I am summoned into Camp Shamrock.

Commandant Evans is waiting for me in his office. He does not invite me to sit. Nor does he offer me coffee. 'Did you wreck Finnbatt Range, Thomas?' I think about it for a millisecond. Then my Cadet School training kicks in. Always tell the truth. I look him in the eye and simply say, 'Yes Sir, I wrecked Finnbatt Range.'

Commandant Evans shrugs. 'Well, Ops are going nuts about it. I've to give you a severe talking to. It was described to me by the Finnish Battalion Executive Officer as – and I quote – "A Three Ring Circus". According to the Finn's Report, "The Irish shooting contingent arrived at 0800 and fed everyone in the Wadi. They then removed some of their clothings [sic] and fired approximately 12,000 rounds of ammunition. Violently."

'Is this a true and accurate account of what happened, Thomas?' he asks.

'Eh, yes Sir, that about sums it up.'

Commandant Evans looks at me. 'For some reason, the Finnish Minister has personally called the Battalion Commander and complimented us on your knowledge of Irish literature. He says you are a great ambassador for Ireland. I don't exactly know what went on up there, Thomas. And I don't want to know. I've given you your talking to. Any questions?' I reply in the negative. Commandant Evans, now smiling, invites me to join him for coffee. It looks like I'm still going to get to Damascus.

# Chapter 20

# Calvin Klein Spring Collection

*Insha'Allah. It is the will of Allah that his donkey die in A Company*

The following day, Hizbullah begin yet another series of savage attacks on the compounds throughout Irishbatt's AO. Tuesday, 9 January sees them hit the Cuckoo's Nest near Rshaf. DFF 13 retaliates and is joined by all of the firebases throughout our AO. The attacks continue with three successive waves of attacks by Hizbullah on Sunday, 14 January. Despite their casualties – the battered corpses whom we are collecting on a daily basis – Hizbullah seem emboldened. In the early hours of Monday, 15 January, Hizbullah target a six-man Israeli foot patrol with an Improvised Explosive Device (IED) in the village of At Tiri. The Israelis sustain casualties and we watch the medevac from the ridgeline across the wadi. Once the Israeli choppers have swung back over Israeli territory, heading south and east for Ram Bam Hospital in Haifa, the Firebases begin their retaliation. Aside from the 360-degree sweep of probing fire, shelling and tracer rounds, the Israelis also begin offensive patrols into the villages around their positions.

On 16 January, the IDF enter At Tiri supported by a Merkava main battle tank. It crushes cars, knocks down walls and destroys a number of olive groves in the village. Some of the gnarled olive trees – I learn later –

152

have been there for hundreds of years. The elderly residents of At Tiri are terrified. There are no young people there as they have all fled to Beirut to escape the violence. Only the elderly remain. They stare at their pitiful and pathetic belongings strewn about the village which has been systematically sacked by the Israeli and South Lebanese Army patrol. We patrol into the village after the fact in order to report the damage. Not surprisingly, some of the villagers are openly hostile. We are a day late and a dollar short.

The cycle of violence continues. The following day, Hizbullah score a direct hit on an Israeli M113 Armoured Personnel Carrier with a Sagger missile. The attack happens near Bayt Yahun. The Israelis and their proxies swarm around the burning M113 and pull the dead and injured out. The ammunition inside the APC then begins to detonate or 'cook off'. After the subsequent medevac, as the choppers dust off the ground and sway and groan in widening circles towards Israeli airspace, the customary retaliation begins. Thousands of rounds of heavy machine gun fire is directed into Bayt Yahun. We are called to evacuate the remaining Lebanese civilians. The elderly residents of Bayt Yahun are traumatized. One old couple have sustained serious head wounds. The man is silent. His head downcast as blood rolls off his chin and pools at his feet in the Sisu. His wife is lying on a stretcher. She is unconscious.

I'm wondering what the cumulative effect of this will have on us. Apart from feeling very fucking fidgety, I think I'll be OK. No shaking hands. But, the Bingo sessions in Al Yatun are very loud affairs. I start really looking forward to those nights when I'm not on patrol. When I don't have to go out the long straight road to the Cuckoo's Nest. When, instead I can horse down a bottle of Kefraya with green thing and white thing and chicken in a flak jacket. And then knock back a few fiery whiskeys. Jameson is our favourite. To take the edge off things. Never mind the hangover the next day. I foolishly congratulate myself. No negative side effects detected.

We wake up to snow in the AO on Wednesday, 18 January. The snow lies silent and eerie white across the post. Some of the A Company troops are goofing around throwing snowballs. I havn't seen snow like this since primary school in Dublin in the 1970s.

After a week of heavy snow, night patrols are unbelievably cold. I've got a series of layers on me. Thermals, combats, Gore-Tex, flak jacket, and on top of that, a parka jacket. Wollen skip cap under the helmet. Two pairs of gloves. Standing up in the back hatch, I get brain freeze from the cold wind in my face. Cruel stars overhead glittering in the icy black. I squat and try to lean towards the grilles over the engine compartment. Getting some warmth there.

A thaw sets in on Sunday, 21 January. Filthy meltwater everywhere. Dripping off the billets. Mucky pools on the floors of all the portakabins. Water percolating through the rocks and sandy soil and leeching into the bunkers underground. Everything is wet and miserable. If anything, it feels colder than when we had the snow.

Hizbullah attack Brashit Compound that morning at 11 AM. There is, yet again, the predictable response. Right through midday and into the late afternoon and gathering darkness, the Compounds pour a steady stream of automatic fire and artillery into the Area of Operations. The villages close down. Families huddle in the darkness of cellars and basements. We continue to observe, monitor and record all of the firing incidents. Sending report after report to the UN in New York. I am increasingly aware that none of this is reported at home in Ireland. The Irish public are blissfully unaware of the ongoing attacks in Irishbatt.

On that same day in Ireland, Senator George Mitchell publishes the eponymous Mitchell Report, which will become a corner stone of the Irish Peace Process. Mitchell's input will bring an end to the cycle of violence in Ireland. A conflict which in part prompted me to join the army. In its own strange way, the violence in Ireland has led me to Lebanon. During the morning, Hafif tells me that Senator George Mitchell's mother, Mary Saad is from Bkassine, Lebanon. And, also, almost unbelievably, Senator Mitchell's father, originally of Irish descent, was orphaned and then adopted by a Lebanese family in Maine. The Lebanese regard Mitchell as one of their own. I am constantly surprised by the deep links between Ireland and Lebanon and the search for peace in both countries. If a Lebanese can bring peace to Ireland – can the Irish bring peace to Lebanon? BS Begley laughs at the idea. 'Peace? Our mission is to get home in one piece. That's the only piece you should be interested in.'

The following day, Hizbullah detonate a major roadside bomb deep inside the Israeli controlled area. The IED is on a track just west of Houle. Several IDF and local pro-Israeli militia are injured. Some have catastrophic injuries including limb separation. The Israelis seem rattled by the infiltration so deep into their territory. It is apparent to us all that Hizbullah are becoming ever more effective in their attacks on the IDF. In terms of body count, the armed struggle seems more evenly matched. What the Ops staff at Battalion Headquarters refer to as the 'exchange ratio' in terms of dead and injured on either side, is approaching 1:1. This is an unacceptable attrition rate for the Israelis. The scene is set for a serious escalation of violence. In Irishbatt, we are briefed over and over again in this regard. We seek to enhance our force protection measures. We check our flak jackets and ballistic plates. We inspect our Kevlar helmets for any tiny cracks and exchange them for new ones with the Logs

Officer. We are constantly checked to make sure we are carrying our dog tags and identity discs. The emphasis is placed once more on tying them to our belt loops. No explanation required at this stage.

The Medical Officer chirpily informs us at one brief that we have received large stocks of blood and plasma products.

Down in the villages on our patrol routes, the call to prayer increases in frequency and pitch. Ramadan starts on 22 January. As the Israelis evacuate their dead and injured from Houle and as we watch their choppers clatter south and east towards Israel, the Muezzin's plaintive call echoes up to us from Haris.

On Tuesday, 23 January, a dramatic new development places the entire Battalion on alert. In a serious and sinister escalation in the tit-for-tat violence, the Israelis enter the village of Rshaf in four M113 armoured personnel carriers. We observe the tracked vehicles skirting the Cuckoo's Nest and entering the tiny hamlet of narrow cobbled lanes and small villas – battered and bruised from years of shelling and small arms fire. The M113s are joined by a ten-man Israeli foot patrol from the Cuckoo's Nest. We then observe a number of heavily armed men in civilian clothing dismount from the Israeli vehicles. Whilst the Israeli soldiers fan out and provide a defensive screen and outer cordon, the men in civilian clothing begin hammering on doors and calling out in Arabic. After a while, a small crowd of mostly elderly residents have been corralled in the central square. As we watch and are frantically raising the matter with Observer Group Lebanon and UNIFIL Headquarters, matters deteriorate. The armed men separate out four women and take them at gunpoint to one of the APCs. They then take three young men at gunpoint and frogmarch them to the other APC. Through our binoculars and scopes, the scene is vivid but played out in silence like a black and white movie. The older residents are clearly upset at the sight of their sons and daughters being abducted at gunpoint.

The APCs withdraw from the village and head towards Rumaysh and an Israeli position known as Gate 08. We later learn that the men and women have been detained at the infamous interrogation centre at Khiam.

Hizbullah's attacks continue unabated and the final week of January sees a concentration of further attacks on the Cuckoo's Nest at DFF 13, the Haddathah Compound at DFF 17 and the Brashit Compound at DFF 23. All of these firebases are in the Irishbatt Area of Operations. The Israeli backlash intensifies and we continue to extract bodies from the wadis. None of this is reported at home.

I manage to get my father on the phone at the end of January. 'You're having a fine time out there I suppose?' he states more than asks. 'Does it get cold at night?' He tells me about night duty in Dublin's city centre in the 1950s. 'It gets very cold at about 4 or 5 in the morning,' he informs me. I agree it is cold. I tell him we have been very busy. Down the crackling phone line he comments 'That's good, the time will fly in.' My mother is not at home. 'You'll see her soon enough,' are his parting words. I try to call my girlfriend in the remaining ninety seconds allotted to me. The queue outside is restless when they hear me hang up and dial again. The number rings out. The answering machine tells me that the message box is full.

The next morning after breakfast I encounter Khalid lurking in the bar area behind the counter. He is eating a tub of chocolate yoghurt. Eating being an understatement. He is wolfing it. He even has a chocolate moustache. 'What about Ramadan?' I ask him. He looks at me in genuine astonishment. 'You don't really believe in all that shit do you?' he asks incredulously.

Psycho interrupts us over the PA system. 'BMR Duty Officer to the

Checkpoint. I say again, Bedridden Mobile Reserve . . . Duty Officer to the Checkpoint.' It doesn't sound urgent and I make my way out to the gate. There, across the cattle grid, in the centre of the checkpoint lies a donkey. He looks distressed. He is lying on his side and breathing heavily, flecks of foam bubbling at his mouth. The A Company personnel on checkpoint duty are gently removing the ancient tack and saddle bags from him. The donkey is blocking the road, lying right between the tank stops. A queue of cars is building up. Horns are honking. The Corporal in charge of the checkpoint is trying to calm an elderly Lebanese man – the donkey's owner – who is talking and shouting animatedly in Arabic.

The guys drag the saddle bags over to one side. They then scramble to one side of the donkey and are trying to figure out how to get him off the road. The one I recognise as Mad Bastard has taken control of the situation. 'Right, on three – we heave 'em over this way.' The Corporal breaks away from the old man and shouts out further instructions. 'Don't fuckin' heave him into the post. Heave him over to Hafif's shop. We've enough fucking donkeys in Al Yatun already.'

Hafif comes running on to the checkpoint. 'Jazes, lads, Jazes' he shouts, 'I don't want dis fuckin' donkey either.'

Eventually the lads heave and haul the unfortunate donkey onto Hafif's 'veranda.' Hafif disappears inside cursing darkly.

The Corporal has persuaded the old man to sit down on one of the plastic bucket seats next to Hafif's veranda and is shouting inside for Chai. Or coffee. Hafif obliges. The old man recovers somewhat.

'What's in them saddlebags?' asks the Corporal.

'That is secret,' replies the old man.

The Corporal points to me. 'Will you tell the officer there what's in the bags? He won't tell anyone. Scouts honour.' He winks at me. The old man beckons me over with his bony finger.

'*Ahlan wa sahlan* Sadiki,' I greet him. The old man beckons me closer and looks around him conspiratorially – checking for eavesdroppers. His face is brown and lined like a sultana. His eyes flash with energy and wit. One eye has a plasma blast. I gather myself together. 'What's in the saddlebags?' I ask him, 'Eh, *les panniers. Quest que dans les panniers?*'

His eyes widen. 'You are fucking French?' he asks me. He spits contemptuously into the dirt.

'No, Irish,' I reply.

He relents. 'Well, I will tell you what is in the bags then. It is Calvin Klein Spring Collection.' The Corporal whistles. Hafif pours the coffee and one eyebrow is raised at the mention of Calvin Klein.

Hafif takes over the interrogation. 'What you mean, Calvin Klein Spring Collection?' He rattles off a question in Arabic. The old man drinks the coffee and clearing his throat, spits generously into the road. 'Yes, Calvin Klein. Spring Collection.' His voice becomes urgent. He looks at each one of us solemnly. 'Not yet in Paris. Not yet in Milan. Not yet in New York.' He then stands up shakily and points his index finger at the ancient saddle bags. 'But here, in Al Yatun. Exclusive for you.'

Hafif eyes him speculatively. 'There ye are now,' observes the Corporal. I ask the old man how he has managed this exclusive. He fingers his beard thoughtfully. He scrutinizes me carefully as he contemplates what he obviously considers to be an impudent question.

'You are small man, but I will take you into my heart.' Eyes flashing he then declares, 'Calvin Klein is my personal friend.'

'Well, well now,' observes the Corporal. 'Well, that fuckin' explains everything.'

An hour or so later, some relatives of the old guy arrive and heft the donkey onto the back of a pickup truck. There is much beeping of horns and embracing at the checkpoint as the old guy heads off in triumph. He has sold approximately half of Calvin Klein's Spring Collection to the lads drifting in and out of Hafif's shop. Hafif is philosophical. 'Insha'Allah. It is the will of Allah that his donkey die in A Company. The Dublin soldier, he is spending money. That old man is lucky his donkey didn't die in B Company. Them culchies are the stingiest fuckers in Irishbatt.' Hafif has learned all of his English from the Dubs. It shows.

# Chapter 21

# February

*78 Irishbatt Operations Summary February 1996*
*Shooting Incidents: 203, Firings Close to Irishbatt Positions: 23, Serious*
*Incidents involving armed elements: 8, Air Incursions by Israeli Aircraft: 4*
Unit History, 78 Irishbatt, UNIFIL

A depression tracks east, north of the Libyan coastline towards Lebanon. It brings the Khamsin, or warm wind heavily laden with dust and sand from the Sahara. Spring has arrived early in Al Yatun. And unlike Ireland, South Lebanon actually has a Spring. The weather improves dramatically in the first week of February. Flowers spring up all over the wadis. The goat herds with their flocks meander along the rocky stony pathways. Scenes from the Bible. It reminds me of the illustrations of the Holy Land in my catechism in St Canice's National School in Finglas in the 1970s. Pastoral scenes. Usually the illustrations in my school books were of cute little lambs. Lambs held by kindly looking bearded men. I have not seen any lambs or sheep in the AO though. Just goats. And you smell them before you see them. And the beardy guys with them normally curse at us.

So, the Khamsin drops thousands of tons of dust and sand and grit into Irishbatt. It gets everywhere. Into your clothes, mouth, eyes. It is swept into the billets and portakabins by the warm wind. It is permanently underfoot. And in the late afternoon, the dust haze turns the sun a vivid glowing red. A fiery orb descending low over the Israeli Compounds directly opposite us on the edge of the Wadi Saluki. The dust gets into the vehicles and clogs our weapons. I get the troops to clean their weapons twice daily. To make sure that the cocking mechanisms are smooth. BS Begley inspects the weapons on the Sisus continuously. Corporal Kennedy is not impressed. 'We never fuckin' fire the fuckin' cannons. What's the point?' He then perks up. 'Except for that day when you, personally oversaw the fuckin' destruction of Finnbatt range.'

The first week of February is quiet. And apart from the sandstorm – uneventful. And then, on Monday, 5 February, Hizbullah re-commences its coordinated attacks on the Israeli compounds in Irishbatt. This time, they attack Compounds DFF 20A and DFF 20 near Bayt Yahun. The attack takes place under cover of darkness and we watch with interest as Hizbullah manoeuvre closer and closer to the perimeter walls of the compounds. The Israelis are responding – as usual – with what we term euphemistically 'maximum exploitation of firepower'. Irishbatt's AO during these firefights becomes a de facto free fire zone. We log all of the shots and report it up the chain of command to the UN in Naqoura. They in turn report it to UN Headquarters in New York. For the local Lebanese, Christians and Muslims alike, moderates or whatever, parents, farmers, workers, whomsoever – the trick to staying alive is not to get shot or blown to bits during one of the attacks. And that simply means, not getting caught in the open. Easier said than done.

And the locals do get killed. Innocent civilians. Usually the elderly and infirm who can't move fast enough into the cellar or whatever improvised shelter a family are using. And also the kids. Who are out playing and don't have the sense to get down when the rounds go off. Sometimes, people just out in their cars driving from A to B get caught in the firefight. They end up getting shot or shelled quite often.

And I am struck at how none of this is reported at home in the Irish media. We get the news digest from Ireland daily. A printout of the main headlines. Lebanon is never mentioned. It puzzles me greatly. Especially when I see the local kids going to school in the mornings as we patrol past them. Dressed in their uniforms – just like the kids I used to teach in Lucan. But, in Lucan, it might be raining. Unlike here where the unspeakable can – and does – happen. We often talk about it amongst ourselves while on patrol. The troops are of the view that the army doesn't want anyone in Ireland to be worried about us. 'If that is the case,' concludes Corporal Kennedy, 'then it's workin', cos no one at home gives a fuck about us. My mot thinks I'm just gettin' a suntan.'

Hizbullah's attacks continue relentlessly. During February, Hizbullah settle into a rhythm. On average, for every seventy-two hours they launch at least one major coordinated attack within Irishbatt's Area of Operations. Things continue to heat up. The number of shooting incidents increases to over 200. Irishbatt positions suffer direct hits from artillery almost every day. Psycho announces over the PA, 'Attention all personnel, Gate 12 has opened fire again. Get me off this rubble.' It is a miracle that no one is killed.

Corporal Smith asks me if we are making a difference. The guys look at me with interest as I try to reply. Try to justify what we are doing. 'Eh, well, we are the eyes and ears of the world. We are the witnesses to the conflict. If we weren't here, the gloves would come off. And a lot more people would get killed.'

Corporal Kennedy gives me a slow handclapping round of applause. 'Great fuckin' speech.'

BS Begley observes drily. 'Corporal Smith, age nineteen. You are not going to bring peace to the Middle East any time soon. So, keep the head down. The object of the exercise here is to get home in one piece.'

Corporal Smith replies earnestly. 'If my kids ask me did I ever kill any-one when I was in the army, I'll tell them that I saved peoples lives. And if I saved one life. Like that old woman up in Rshaf. Then that'll have made it all worthwhile.'

Corporal Kennedy is clearly gobsmacked at Corporal Smith's sincer-ity. 'Would ye listen to Mother fuckin' Teresa there.' Unfortunately, the nickname sticks. Corporal Smith, formerly known as Minus is now known as Mother Teresa. I know I would have made exactly the same speech when I was his age. But now things aren't as black and white to me.

The Force Commander, a Polish General, visits the Irish Battalion during the first week of February. There is a frenzy of whitewashing and tidying up in the run up to his visit. The taciturn Pole arrives and makes a speech. Corporal Kennedy mimics his speech with a passable imperson-ation of Pope John Paul the Second. 'My brothers and seesters of Irishbatt – we luff you.' For some reason, news of the Force Commander's visit reaches Ireland. Somehow, a picture appears in the newspapers at home of Irish troops wearing the ridiculous blue cravats and standing to attention in the blinding sunlight in Camp Shamrock. To add insult to injury, my Mum cuts out the picture and sends it 3000 miles back to Al Yatun. She writes, 'Your camp looks lovely. And those cravats are lovely too. It looks like a lovely day. You must be having a lovely time.'

I'm reading her letter as the ground shakes around me during another round of attack and counter attack on Haddathah Compound. The cockroaches are falling off the ceiling and landing on me and around me. Wriggling and scuttling away. I don't even bother to squash them any-more. Khalid asks me if the letter is from my 'sweetheart'. 'Ehh, no, my mother,' I reply.

'Do you have picture of her?' he asks eagerly. I think something may have got lost in translation. I show him a photo of my girlfriend. He is entranced.

'This is your mother?' he asks.

'Eh, no, my girlfriend.' Khalid looks disappointed. 'You should get Chinese girlfriend. They are best for working and shut up.' I wonder how many Chinese women Khalid has ever met. Khalid then breaks the spell of our enchanting interlude on romance and related matters. He announces loudly: 'Chicken in flak jacket, green things and spuds for dinner.'

Despite the ongoing attacks, and despite the Force Commander's inspection, the Battalion Commander insists on another inspection on 13 February. More whitewashing, polishing and general bullshit is the order of the day. I observe Sergeant Fuckin-Fuck moving through the billets organising work parties. More dirty details. Some of the stone gabions are emptied and refilled again. 'The fuckin' devil makes work for idle fuckin' hands' is Sergeant Fuckin-Fuck's pithy comment as I pass him.

Luckily for me I miss the Battalion Commander's inspection. I'm up in Bayt Yahun with the Sisus – providing an armoured escort for a humanitarian medical clinic. It has been set up by arrangement with the Muktar. The Medical Officer eats an apple on the way up to Bayt Yahun. A TCD graduate, he is on a short service commission and will return to hospital medicine in Ireland or the UK on his return. 'This is more interesting than the NHS,' he remarks as the Sisu passes through the Israeli gates and enters the Israeli Controlled Area.

He treats dozens, mostly elderly men and women in the village. And, a young woman with a tiny infant. BS Begley is unsettled when he sees the baby. 'Who'd have a baby in this God forsaken place?' he asks me. He seems angry. We gather whatever dollars we have and give them to the young woman. She looks away and hands the money to an old woman.

She gives us a toothless grin and moves – fairly nimbly – down the narrow alley and out of sight. As we are leaving, the old woman and some of her neighbours approach us from the alley. All elderly, with incredibly dark eyes and lined faces. They are carrying flowers which they have cut from their terraces. They give us bread and olives. We feel guilty receiving the gifts. BS Begley warns the lads to look grateful. 'This is all they have.' The flowers look out of place in the Sisu. They remind me of my mother. They remind me of home. That's it, I think. It's official. I'm homesick. I'm sick of the all-male environment. I miss normal life. I miss my girlfriend. Corporal Kennedy takes me out of my reverie, however.

As we are leaving the village, I notice Corporal Kennedy leering at me from the other side of the APC. He calls over to me over the noise of the engine, cupping his hands around his mouth. 'You like them oul' wans didn't ye?' He is grinning at me now. 'Let me tell ye now. Them oul' wans would cut your fuckin' throat if ye turned yer back on them for even a split second. Did ye see the one with the mad eyes? She's a natural born fuckin' killer that one.'

Even BS Begley is shocked. 'You need a break, Corporal Kennedy. Maybe you should go to Damascus with Lieutenant Clonan.' The BS digs me in the ribs. 'You could be his bodyguard. Keep him out of trouble with the Pipe Band.' Corporal Kennedy's eyes light up with a feral glow. 'That's fuckin deadly.' I realise to my horror, that he is the only Corporal in the BMR who has a full army driving permit. He is also the only one who hasn't been outside the Area of Operations since we arrived. It looks like we'll be discovering the delights of Syria together.

The following week, the Israelis attack the village of Majdal Silm with helicopter gunships. The A Company troops at Al Jurn hear the Apache helicopters before they see them. The choppers emerge thumping and whopping out of the Wadi Saluki – having used it for cover during their approach from the direction of Markabe to the east. They circle Majdal silm popping flares and firing out sheets of metallic chaff. One of the choppers remains at a few thousand feet, circling slowly and providing top cover for the other aircraft. The second chopper swoops low and adopts a holding position over the village. We are watching this unfold from the road between Tibnine and As Sultaniyah. The hovering chopper begins the usual pattern – firing the bushmaster heavy machine gun into houses. Reducing them to rubble. They fire a Tow missile. We see the puff of smoke. Later we hear a whoosh and then the rolling thunder as the missile detonates inside someone's living room. Suddenly, the chopper bucks violently and roars sideways, almost belly up, desperately attempting to gain altitude. We hear a new sound. Someone on the ground is firing a heavy machine gun at the chopper. We discover later that Hizbullah have pre-positioned a vehicle-mounted anti-aircraft weapon in the area on the off-chance of a low flying, slow-moving target such as this. We hear the steady thump thump thump of the anti-aircraft gun. The tracer rounds are unmistakable as they sail gracefully up in a fountain of fire from the olive groves below.

The second chopper saturates the area with fire. The pilots rapidly ascend and veer east towards Israel. This is a new development for Hizbullah. The incident challenges the heretofore undisputed air superiority of the Israelis within the area of operations. Ironically, Hizbullah have eschewed state of the art 'smart' shoulder launched weapons in favour of old fashioned direct fire anti-aircraft guns. The Israelis had developed too many electronic countermeasures for the fire and forget weapons that are laser guided or wire guided. So, Hizbullah have resorted back to the tried and tested method of firing along line of sight at the target. The main disadvantage being that the firer is vulnerable to immediate counter attack and suppressing fire. Or in other words, almost certain death. This does not seem to faze Hizbullah. The Israelis will think twice about sending helicopters into the villages in future. Indeed, within minutes of the attack, a pair of Israeli jets – fast moving, high altitude aircraft – arrive on station and fire a number of 500lb bombs into Majdal Silm. As usual, we observe, note and record. Then, in the coming hours and days, we move in and remove the dead and injured. The 500lb bombs leave a crater where a house once stood. No trace of the building.

Ramadan ends on 21 February. The villages throughout Irishbatt celebrate Eid-al-fitr. In the warm evenings, young people walk the roads, tracks and boithrins of the AO. Girls on one side of the road, boys on the other. Dressed to the nines. Tommy Hilfiger jeans and designer sunglasses. They are mostly teenagers from Beirut visiting their relatives down south. Many are from the United States. Visiting the old country. They smile and wave at us as we patrol past them. The girls giggle and smile shyly at us. Some of the younger boys run alongside the Sisus and high five us. Warm hands gripped briefly in the twilight. They are like teenagers anywhere in the world. With Nike and Reebok trainers. Designer T-Shirts. Just like the Israeli teenagers I saw on Jaffa Street in Jerusalem. Or on the seafront at Netanyiah.

Once the celebrations of Eid are over, Hizbullah resume their attacks on the Israeli compounds once more. I get another letter from Ireland. In this, my Dad has cut out another picture of the Irish Battalion being inspected by the CO. More blue cravats and soldiers standing to attention in Camp Shamrock. As though they were at home in Ireland. On parade. My Dad writes, 'Lots of spit and polish it seems. You must have plenty of time on your hands.'

Later that evening, on 28 February, the Israelis move into the village of At Tiri to carry out a punitive operation against the elderly inhabitants there. They are obviously fed up with the continuous attacks on the

Cuckoo's Nest and Haddathah Compound. These attacks do not originate in At Tiri. This doesn't seem to bother the IDF. An eight-man IDF patrol leave compound One Nine Alpha just south of At Tiri and move into the village. They move from house to house firing as they go. Assault rifles and machine guns are fired through the ground floor windows of houses as they move through the narrow alleys. High velocity bullets ripping through ancient wooden shutters and glass into the dark interiors of people's homes. They lob grenades through the smashed windows. A Merkava tank moves to the edge of the village to provide fire support for the foot patrol. It fires high explosive rounds at the village water hole. The soldiers destroy the ancient gnarled olive trees outside people's houses and throw clothing and possessions on to the street. In effect, they sack the village. Flammable liquid is poured on the clothes hanging on clotheslines. Their pathetic few possessions burned. Eventually, the Israelis withdraw.

Hizbullah respond on the leap year date of 29 February. They assault Brashit Compound. And the cycle of violence continues. I get a telephone call from Ireland. It is my girlfriend. She's tired, yawning down the line. Thousands of miles away over static and hiss. Then, apropos nothing, 'Why don't you move in with me when you get back from the Lebanon?'

# Chapter 22

# We're Only Prawns

*78 Irishbatt Operations Summary February 1996*
*Shooting Incidents: 254, Firings Close to Irishbatt Positions: 18, Serious*
*Incidents involving armed elements: 22, Air Incursions by Israeli Aircraft: 7*

Unit History, 78 Irishbatt, UNIFIL

March brings even warmer weather. Spring is firmly established in Lebanon. We ditch the heavily lined Parkas that we've worn all winter. It's even warm on night patrols now. The mosquitoes have returned and I'm eaten alive. Their constant whine as they dance around the periphery of my vision is driving me nuts. BS Begley advises me to drink more whiskey and Almaza; 'It puts them off.'

UAVs are also constantly whining and buzzing around. Israeli unmanned aerial vehicles (UAVs) or drones are a new daily feature. If you stop and listen, they are just about audible, buzzing away overhead somewhere. But they're hard to spot. Corporal Smith, or Mother Teresa, has a talent for pointing them out to us. Underneath his helmet, his glasses glinting in the strong sunlight, he scans the air around us as we patrol, spotting drones. 'Like a hen looking into a bottle,' observes Sergeant Bracken. Every now and then, Corporal Smith exclaims when he spots a particular variant of UAV. He even produces a magazine which contains bright, glossy illustrations of each type of drone – complete with all of the specifications. 'Put the fuckin' *Beano* away, will ye?' Sergeant Bracken teases him. But, we are secretly impressed with his ability to pick out the drones high overhead. We imagine a UAV operator, tracking our movements on a laptop somewhere in an air conditioned bunker in Israel. We take turns giving the fingers in its general direction.

On the 3rd of March, a suicide bomber kills nineteen innocent Israelis on a bus in Jerusalem.

On 4 March, Hizbullah assault the Cuckoo's Nest and Haddathah Compounds in simultaneous attacks. The attacks commence just before nine in the evening. Hizbullah fire mortars from behind the ridgeline to our rear and rake each position with heavy machine gun fire. They put in their ground assault as the perimeters and parapets are getting hammered. Hizbullah have learned that this suppressing fire gives them precious minutes to assault on to the firebases before those inside can recover themselves and get their weapons systems operating.

That short window of opportunity also gives us a chance to take cover from the inevitable 360 degree fire-storm that is going to erupt from the compounds. Just as Haddathah Compound opens up, we manage to lurch bounce and clatter the Sisus into some dead ground west of Haddathah. We'll stay in this dip until the firing has died down. If we climb up the ridgeline towards Haris and the safety of Al Yatun, we'll get caught in the cross fire. I listen to the urgent radio traffic between B Company and Battalion Headquarters as they call the shots that are landing in and around their positions. Thick and heavy. We all grin when we see the red flares popping up from B Company Headquarters. 'That's the end of Monday night Bingo in Haddathah,' remarks Sergeant Bracken.

After an hour or so, the firing begins to ease off. We call in our sentries who have taken up defensive positions around our own vehicles. We head up the track towards Haris and make a right turn heading to Camp Shamrock to refuel the Sisus. I still don't like being around Battalion Headquarters unless absolutely necessary. Too many senior officers knocking around the place with time on their hands. We pass the sentries on the gate. Exchanging insults as we head towards the fuel pumps. The Quartermaster in charge of the POL (Petrol, Oil and Lubricants) depot is friendly and efficient. He's got the huge rubber hose out as we approach. He motions for me and Sergeant Bracken to dismount and have some coffee. We sit on filthy plastic garden furniture. There is oil everywhere and the Quartermaster pours coffee from a pot boiling on a Damascus heater inside his office. The coffee scalds. Its bitterness drowns out the background smell of oil, lubricants and fuel. I've never had a more comfortable seat. Never a better coffee in any restaurant or fancy café terrace. Nor, I think, have I ever had better company than my comrades in arms. The Quartermaster lights a cigarette and flicks the match over the sign which reads 'No Naked Lights.'

As the Sisus are being filled with diesel we chat about the trip. The old timers reckon that this is one of the busiest deployments we've had in Lebanon. As we chew the fat, Commandant Molloy approaches us from the shadows. Out for his evening constitutional. He scans the group and spots me. He calls me over.

'Ah, Lieutenant Cloonan. Can you explain to me why you are incorrectly dressed in Camp?' I'm taken aback.

'Incorrectly dressed, Sir?' I reply. He is carrying his swagger stick. And with it, he pokes at my flak jacket. The zip on the utility pouch at the front is open. Apparently, I've committed the egregious error of entering Camp Shamrock with a pocket left unzipped. I experience an almost uncontrollable urge to take the swagger stick, break it in two and shove the pointy bits up his fat arse. While I'm struggling to retain control,

Sergeant Bracken interrupts the conversation. 'You'll need to sign for the fuel, Sir.' This distracts me sufficiently.

'No problem,' I reply thickly. I'm enraged. When I turn around, Commandant Molloy is still standing there. Smiling insouciantly at me and staring me down. Obviously enjoying his power trip. Apart from ingratiating himself with the Battalion Commander at every available opportunity, his sole mission in life seems to be in bullying those junior officers who have the misfortune to enter his orbit. I thank my lucky stars that I'm in Al Yatun – as far as possible from the habitat of this particular creeping Jesus.

We mount the vehicles. As we drive past him, over the speed ramps, Molloy calls out to me. 'I'm watching you Cloonan. Pray you don't fuck up on my watch.' He has his swagger stick stuck under his arm. He looks like Colonel Blimp.

When we pass under the barrier at the entrance to the camp, Sergeant Bracken turns to look at me. 'There's less to him than meets the eye,' he shouts. When I don't laugh, Sergeant Bracken looks concerned. He leans towards me again and shouts over the roar of the diesel engines as they clatter through the low gears. 'That fucker bothered you didn't he? You take this shit far too seriously. I have my own method for dealing with army bullshit. I call it Planet of the Apes. Basically, when I put on my army uniform, I think, OK, now I'm on the set of *Planet of the Apes*. And anything that happens in uniform, everything that happens in the Army is a scene from *Planet of the Apes*. I just go with the flow. I'm an actor in a play. And when I get home and take off the uniform, I'm back in the real world again. Simple. You'd better get used to the idea, or you're gonna go fuckin' nuts.' He has a point.

Corporal Kennedy looks at Sergeant Bracken with some skepticism. 'Give that man a banana,' he quips.

On 5 March, a suicide bomber kills twelve innocent Israelis in Tel Aviv.

Hizbullah's attacks continue apace through March. Irishbatt sees repeated attacks on the all of the usual suspects. The Cuckoo's Nest, Haddathah Compound and Brashit Compound. The retaliatory fire follows the usual pattern. On 14 March, Gate 12 opens fire without warning and shells Haris and Al Yatun. A total of thirty-nine high-explosive 155mm shells crash into and around the village of Haris. Al Yatun is hit. Mercifully, unbelievably, no one in 6-40 is physically hurt. The villagers are not so lucky. Two men and two women – caught in the open whilst working in the fields below our position – are taken to the hospital in Tibnine after the attack. The locals take them in a convoy of cars. Horns blaring, lights flashing. We receive a Shellwarning from the Israelis a full ten minutes after the firing is over. When challenged by Irishbatt as to the cause for the shelling – no reason is given. It is to be our first taste of indiscriminate, unprovoked fire on our positions. It ups the ante considerably.

When the firing has subsided, we go to the roof to survey the damage. The all clear is sounded. The BMR gets the go-ahead from the Israelis to assist in the evacuation of the wounded. I watch from the roof as the Sisus fire up their engines and head for the gate. As the sentries open the barrier and pull back the tank stops, a 155 round detonates just metres away. The checkpoint is raked with shrapnel. The detonation is deafening. All the more shocking because we hadn't heard it coming. Everyone on the roof crouches down and searches for cover. A red flare is fired from behind us. As it hisses skyward, Sergeant Fuckin-Fuck observes pithily, 'It just goes to show gentlemen. We're only prawns.' And despite the fear and the frustration, we fall about laughing. Prawns indeed.

# Chapter 23

# Don't shoot him now.
# Shoot him on the way back.

*Oh, and by the way, so's you know, everyone, I mean everyone,
calls me Animal now*

On 15 March, we are detailed to attend the Medal Parade in Camp Shamrock. Me and all the other first timers get our UN medals for Lebanon. Mine is pinned to my chest by the Battalion Executive Officer. I'm glad it's him. I spy my nemesis, Commandant Molloy, pinning medals on the ranks of A Company to our left. I'm glad I didn't encounter him.

Immediately after the Medal Parade, I'm summoned along with the other officers to a hurried briefing in the Operations Bunker. The Ops Staff are grim faced. The MIO or Military Intelligence Officer gives us the benefit of his latest contacts with Hizbullah and the Israeli military. 'There's an indication that Hizbullah are planning a major offensive in the coming days and weeks. It's been building up steadily since our arrival in October and the situation has been deteriorating further since Christmas. But, we are expecting things to get a lot worse. How bad things are likely to get, we don't know.' It is decided in this fraught and tense environment to double the number of patrols that the BMR undertake. The idea is to

175

try and inhibit Hizbullah activity in Irishbatt's AO and perhaps dampen down the likelihood of Armageddon in the AO.

That night, my Dad calls to wish me a Happy St Patrick's Day. I tell him about the UN medal. He tells me that it's 'well for you, getting a medal for being in the sun.' He goes on to tell me about the awful weather at home. Our time is rushed. I'm trying to get a sense of what it is like at home. To find out about how my Mum is. Trying to read between the lines. 'Don't be worrying yourself over nothing. You're always worrying,' Dad goes into a fit of coughing. Then I'm cut off.

The following morning at 5 AM myself and Corporal Kennedy hitch a lift down to Camp Shamrock on the Water Truck. Stuffed onto the front bench seat we exchange a lively conversation with Private O'Byrne. She is the only female water truck driver in the Battalion. Every morning after the Early Bird minesweeps and after all routes have been patrolled, she delivers fresh water to all of Irishbatt's positions. She is constantly cheerful. She travels the whole AO every day and never complains. We reckon she should get a special medal of her own. She has her Steyr rifle attached to a rack behind her on the rear window. It's a pretty cool touch we think. It sort of says, 'Don't mess with me – woman with a gun coming through.' We are like a bunch of hillbillies heading into town – the three of us squashed onto the front seat. Corporal Kennedy is in tremendous humour. He's looking forward to Damascus. He has shaved his head almost completely bald for the occasion. Don't ask me why.

We get to Shamrock to pick up the Pipe Band. They too are giddy. Aside from being very talented musicians, the troops from the Pipe Band are assigned to Battalion Headquarters and perform the full range of military duties, such as guarding the camp and other tasks. In addition, they rehearse and perform at all ceremonial occasions that present themselves – such as the medal parade or other VIP visits. They also play many other instruments. A bewildering array, in fact, and all are accomplished traditional Irish musicians. Also, they are all as hard as nails and each as mad as a badger. And it's my job to get them to Damascus – through Israel – and back. In one piece. No injuries. No one to go missing. No arrests. Simple.

While the Pipe Band are loading their instruments into the back of the van, something jumps out at me. Something catches my eye. The sergeant in charge of the band is a stocky, well-built man. He is about my age. And as he heaves the musical instrument cases over the tailgate of the van, his lip is curled up at one end in a sneer that looks familiar. Despite the moustache, I recognise that disgruntled look. I glance at his uniform and see the name Quinn stitched over his pocket. It is like I have been struck by lightning.

'Are you Tommy Quinn?' I ask him.

He stares at me coldly. 'Yeah, why?'

I stick out my hand. 'Tom Clonan. Do you remember? From St Canice's.' His eyes widen. He stares at me again. Closely this time. I remind him, 'Do you remember spitting into Fr Andrew's hat?'

Tommy Quinn exclaims, 'I fuckin' remember you now. You were the guy with the accordion. You got me interested in music.'

Corporal Kennedy watches our reunion from a distance. 'C'mon, will ya. Yis can kiss and make up in the fuckin' van. Let's get outta here.'

Meanwhile, Tommy Quinn can't take his eyes off me. 'How did you end up in the army? How come we didn't meet up before this?' As we climb into the front of the van, Tommy reassures me in a low, serious voice. 'Now, Tom, I've changed a lot since we were kids. Got me act together. The army has sorted me out big time.' I'm glad to hear this. 'Oh, and by the way, so's you know, everyone, I mean everyone, calls me Animal now.' Some things never change it seems.

As Corporal Kennedy slides into the driver's seat of the UN Toyota Minibus, I note once more the gleaming almost bald head. He rubs his hands together with glee and shouts out – 'On the fuckin' road again!' The lads take up the tune. And as we wheel out of the gates of Shamrock – bound for Naqoura and the Israeli border – the lads are roaring their approval. I'm a little unnerved. I'm thinking as Irishbatt recedes into the distance behind us, 'Dear sweet God, please no arrests. Just let me get them to Damascus and back without an international incident.'

We pass through Qana. Then on to Tyre and swinging south through the orange groves and olive groves towards Naqoura. Terraces of vines. You could be fooled into thinking you were in the Rhone Valley. Our armed escort leaves us just South of Tyre as we pass into the Israeli con-trolled area. Two armoured vehicles with French Military Police escort us to the UN position at Naqoura. The Mediterranean glitters out to our right as we head south. I notice several Israeli gunboats just off the coast-line. Narrow, fast-moving, inshore patrol vessels.

We get rid of our weapons in Naqoura as quickly as possible. Corporal Kennedy emerges from a nearby portakabin dressed in a three piece suit. The lads whistle. It is a shiny grey mohair suit to be precise.

'Where the fuck did you get them threads?' asks Animal.

Corporal Kennedy looks a little defensive for a second. Then he replies, 'I got them from Yussuf, the blind Tailor from Tyre.' There is silence. Then laughter all round. 'You'll fuckin' see,' challenges Corporal Kennedy. 'The mots in Damascus will be queuin' up. As the song goes girls, there's nuttin' like a sharp-dressed man. Anyhow, it's too fuckin' late, I've no other civvies with me.' In fact, as I would discover, he had no other anything with him. Not even a toothbrush. A fact which would become ever more obvious over the coming seventy-two hours.

We head south over the border. We go through the same rigmarole with the young Israeli troops at the border crossing point. The search is good natured. The lads exchange robust Dublin humour with the Israeli conscripts in the search area. The English is too fast for them. Animal addresses a young Ukrainian soldier with bulging eyes and sticky-out ears. He looks about fourteen years old. He is swimming in his oversized IDF combats.

'Hey, handsome, do ye have any fuckin' sisters?'

The soldier replies. 'I am not smoking. Sorry.'

I breathe a sigh of relief.

A female Israeli soldier asks the lads to open up the music cases. Animal is a bit put out and grumpily clips open the music cases, 'Oh yeah, like, Ehh, like yer man. Al Capone? Like, I've a fuckin' machine gun in the fiddle case? You've been watchin' too many Godfather videos love.' The female searcher doesn't quite catch the meaning but is smiling. She then frowns when she opens up a case containing a tin whistle. Gently, as though it might contain explosives, she asks Animal to lift it out. Animal obliges and slips the gleaming instrument out of its velvet case. He hands it to the Israeli. She very slowly, gently – as though nervous that there might be a mercury tilt switch inside the tin whistle – lifts it up and rotates it under the strong light above us. The instrument glints and gleams in the glare. She carefully rotates it once more and slowly places the mouthpiece up to her right eye. Squinting up the mouthpiece as though attempting to inspect the inside. Animal gets impatient. 'It's called a fuckin' tin whistle. Have ye not seen one before?' He grabs it from her and blows into the mouthpiece. The loud peep causes everyone to jump. The Ukrainian swings his rifle up from the low port position and points it at me. Corporal Kennedy shouts in alarm. 'Don't fuckin' shoot him now. Shoot him on the way back – we're tryin to get to Damascus.'

# Chapter 24

# St Patrick's Day, Damascus

*I won't be needin' that in Damascus*

We eventually get out of Ros Haniqra and head up the motorway to the Syrian border crossing. The Israelis there are expecting us and do not search us. We cross through the elaborate defensive structure – the last line between Syria and Israel. A no man's land. Marked out by two parallel lines of electrified fence and a sand track. Heavily mined on either side of the sand. The Israelis send armed patrols down the sand track and check for signs of disturbance. They shoot on sight. Not even a lizard could cross the border.

We are met on the other side by the Syrian army. Their checkpoint is filthy. Red and white painted tyres mark out the checkpoint. A tattered Syrian flag flying. A portrait of President Assad inside their border post. Corrugated roofing – gaps in places – over bare, unplastered concrete blocks. The Syrians are all smoking. Their uniforms are dirty. They are irregularly dressed. The officer in charge stares at Corporal Kennedy in his gleaming three piece suit. The suit is even shinier now than his baldy head in the desert sunshine. The Syrian assumes that Corporal Kennedy is in charge due to his extraordinary appearance. Corporal Kennedy rises to the occasion and informs the Syrian that the nature of our visit is to 'Play the pipes for President Gadaffy.'

The Syrian looks confused. 'But, President Assad is President of Syria. Gaddafy is Libya.'

Corporal Kennedy looks blankly at him. 'Eh, yeah. Whatever.' He then asks the Syrian if he knows the best nightclub in Damascus. The Syrian's eyes light up and he and Corporal Kennedy huddle together for several minutes in hushed and urgent conversation. The Syrian writes some names down on a piece of paper and shoves it into Corporal Kennedy's waistcoat pocket. The two embrace as though life-long friends. As we drive off in a plume of dust, Animal roars 'Go on ye good thing ye' at a young Syrian soldier. He waves limply and I breathe another sigh of relief.

As we head north towards Damascus, Corporal Kennedy announces that we are going to the 'Damascus version of Tamangos' tonight. Another cheer from the lads in the back. We drive across the Syrian pan-handle. Occasionally kids come running to the roadside when they see the plume of dust that marks our progress across the rutted tracks and roads. The kids are literally dressed in rags. We stop and give them our dollars. And our water. Corporal Kennedy gives his waistcoat to a scrawny teenager. 'There ye are. I won't be needin' that in Damascus.'

We arrive in Damascus just before dark and check in to the Beit Al Wali Hotel in the Bab Touma district of downtown Damascus. We are met by the UNTSO (United Nations Truce Supervision Organisation) representative in Damascus. We are playing at a concert that night for the ex-pat Irish community in the Damascus Towers Hotel. There will be several high ranking Syrian regime figures attending. We change into uniform and travel in two taxis to the hotel. The guys perform like consummate professionals. Animal leads them up and down the stage playing reels and all manner of martial songs. This gets the crowd going.

The Irish are clearly moved by this reminder of home. The Syrians are on their feet. Shouting encouragement in Arabic at Animal and the lads. The drink is flying. I'm sitting next to a guy with dark glasses and a red fez. He is like something straight out of central casting from a James Bond movie. He reminds me of 'secret man.' I wonder if they are related. We are all getting fairly hammered.

And, then, in a scene reminiscent of every nightclub in every town in Ireland, the music is interrupted at midnight by a loud announcement from the PA. An Irish voice – one of the officers from UNTSO – announces, 'Ladies and Gentlemen, would you please stand for the National Anthem.' And then, over the speakers comes 'Amhrán na bhFiann'. Everyone staggers to their feet. Animal AKA Tommy Quinn is standing stiffly to attention on the stage. Then the lights come on and everyone starts leaving.

Corporal Kennedy sidles up to me. 'We've been invited to play at a party by the hotel manager.' I look over and the hotel manager, bedecked in evening wear and bow tie is winking at us and beckoning us to follow him. We head out to the foyer, and the manager – a Hercule Poirot lookalike – bundles us into two stretch limousines with blacked out windows. Animal is already in the back and has discovered a minibar. We head out of the city centre and up a series of switchbacks to a gated residence high on the hills overlooking the city. We are then escorted into a massive villa. There is a party in full swing. Corporal Kennedy stares at the elaborate chandelier hanging from the centre of the hallway. 'Holy fuckin' sheepshit,' is all he can manage.

We are then ushered into a huge open plan reception. Marble floors. Gleaming gold filigree twisting around black and green marble columns. Waiters with silver trays. The room is packed with revellers. Presumably the upper echelons of Damascus high society. Oh, and us too.

Animal bursts through the crowd and implores me to follow him. 'You won't fuckin' believe this.' We push our way up to the stage. There is a belly dancer swaying to the deafening Arab music. Only, on closer inspection, it is not a woman. It's a man. A big fat man with a hairy chest. Animal is shouting at him, 'Go on ye good thing ye!' Two burly men appear and gently but firmly move us away from the stage. They explain to me in broken English, 'The dancer is President Assad's bastard son. You have to show respect for his dancing.' They are good humoured and pat Animal down. Soothing him with entreaties and offers of a drink. By the time Animal has calmed down, we are joined by Corporal Kennedy and the rest of the band. The bouncers force a passage through the crowd and the lads are hoisted onto the stage.

Assad the dancer flounces off the stage and the lads belt into a series of jigs and reels. The crowd start clapping and for the second time that night the Pipe Band have the crowd on their feet.

There is a sudden commotion and dozens of guys in moustaches and sunglasses enter the ballroom. It is Assad himself and his entourage. The nervous host rushes the stage and makes an effort to announce Assad's arrival. Assad waves him off the stage and claps his hands. 'Music,' he orders, smiling. It occurs to me that I'm looking at a tin-pot dictator. A good old fashioned mass murderer. Animal and the boys tear into 'A Nation Once Again' and then 'The Fields of Athenry.' 'The Fields of Athenry' bring the Syrians to their feet. Me, Corporal Kennedy and Syrians alike wiping tears from our eyes. Assad stands transfixed. He joins in the chorus of 'The Fields'. The evening goes on into the early hours. My last hazy recollection of the villa was of Corporal Kennedy, doing an impromptu Riverdance performance on a large round table. I notice his suit is beginning to wilt a little. The seam on his shoulder has become unstitched and is unravelling.

# Chapter 25

# Animal is Dead

The following morning I awake with the worst hangover I can remember. The minibar in the hotel room is open, its feeble light illuminating a slew of bottles strewn across the carpet. Whiskey, vodka and gin miniatures that Corporal Kennedy and Animal had swigged back the night before in an impromptu 'concert' given in my room. I have a hazy recollection of a group of Syrian hotel workers and a taxi driver clapping and stamping to Animal's pipes in the room. Heaven knows what the other guests thought was going on.

There is a sharp staccato knocking on my door. Corporal Kennedy is outside. 'C'mon Lieutenant Clonan. Are ye alive in there? It's time to go to the Souk.' I crawl out of the bed and throw some water over my face. I fight back a dry heave and as waves of nausea pass through me, I emerge into the blinding sunlight and heat of downtown Damascus. 'Beepity Beeep.' Corporal Kennedy honks the horn of the UN minibus and gives me the thumbs up. Animal is on the front bench seat. He looks like death warmed up. White as a sheet and sweating, he opens the passenger door for me. 'C'mon – we're goin for a Turkish bath. The best bleedin' cure in the Middle East.' Corporal Kennedy steps on the accelerator and we weave in and out of the Damascus rush hour traffic. We abandon the minibus a block away from the Souk. An elderly man with worry beads slides a crash barrier alongside the vehicle and announces with a broad smile, 'Car Park for my American friends.' Corporal Kennedy – who has dispensed with his jacket as 'the fuckin' sleeve came off of it' – replies that we are Irish. 'Good, good. Good price for Russians.' We stumble towards the El-Hamidiyeh Souk.

The entrance to the Souk is dark, cool and inviting. We descend into the old city markets. The stalls within its dark and cavernous interior are filled with spices. The fragrant scents of cardamom, harissa, chermoula, berbere and baharat fill the air.

'Are you sure about this?' I ask Corporal Kennedy as we approach a dark and dirty side-alley. Corporal Kennedy seems to know where he is going and leads us to a dust covered wooden door studded with metal bolts and intricate iron fretwork.

'Don't be worryin' – Assad's bodyguards told me about this place last night. I checked it out meself this morning. You're gonna fuckin' love it.' Corporal Kennedy produces a tatty piece of paper from his wallet and knocks on the door. After some time a grille opens up and suspicious eyes give us the once over. Corporal Kennedy passes the piece of paper through the grille. There is a loud grating noise and bolts are slid back. A large man with a huge moustache beckons us inside. There are more moustachioed men inside who greet us with the traditional '*Ahlan wa sahlan.*' I notice in the dim interior that Animal is even paler than he was outside in the Souk. The main man claps his hands and without further ceremony we are ushered into what turns out to be a changing room of sorts. A disaffected youth appears with some towels. He is also carrying a basket into which he points. 'Everything. Hurry. Now.'

I'm feeling a bit uneasy as we strip down to our boxer shorts. Especially when I put my trousers with my wallet and passport into the wicker basket. 'Everything. Hurry. Now,' repeats the youth.

'Even our jocks?' enquires Corporal Kennedy in disbelief.

'Everything. Hurry. Now,' shrieks the boy. He clears his throat loudly and spits back through the door. We eye each other warily.

Animal says resignedly, 'Let's get it fuckin' over with before I fuckin' keel over.'

With just towels around our waists, we are then led into an inner chamber by the boy. Into a steam filled room which is incredibly hot. Through the steam I can make out a number of benches and massage tables. And also, about a half a dozen large men with a variety of large moustaches. They look like entrants to a Saddam Hussein lookalike competition. They greet us with broad smiles and direct us onto the massage tables. Without further ado, they then pick up what look like palm fronds and begin whipping us on our backs and legs. The whipping of the fronds produces an intense burning and stinging sensation.

'Jazes,' roars Corporal Kennedy. I'm about to object also, when we are ushered into another room. In this room, a fresh group of Saddam Husseins are waiting with what look like brillo pads in buckets of steaming water. They proceed to scrub our backs and legs with a series of abrasive implements. From wire wool scrubbers to what look like large bristling toilet brushes.

And that's when it happens. Animal slides off his massage table and takes a swing at one of the 'masseurs'. He in turn strikes Animal on the crown of his head with the toilet brush implement. It makes a loud and surprisingly hollow 'thock' sound. Animal goes down like a sack of spuds. We jump up and look at him. His eyes are open but worryingly unseeing. Corporal Kennedy makes a quick diagnosis. 'Animal is dead. He's had a heart attack or something. Let's get the fuck out of here. Quick.'

After a heated argument with Corporal Kennedy, I finally persuade him that we cannot abandon Animal to the Saddam Hussein lookalikes. After some hurried negotiation and profuse apologies, I manage to calm the situation. The Saddams are giving Animal daggers looks the whole time. They help us to carry him out through a side door and into the Souk itself. The sudden waft of cold air revives Animal. The Saddams are trying to retrieve their towels and a crowd is assembling around us. We are now faced with the prospect of being ejected, naked, penniless and without passports into the Souk. I think of the Battalion Executive Officer's prophetic warning to me before we left Camp Shamrock. 'Cloonan [sic], don't fuck up.' I swallow hard and try not to think of the consequences.

Eventually, thankfully, the disaffected youth appears once more and empties the basket containing our clothes on the cobbles around us. We hastily dress and escape from the enthusiastic crowd who are closing in on us and shouting things in Arabic whose meaning I shudder to think of if they were translated.

When we get back to the minibus, we pay off the old guy. We then go through our belongings. Thankfully, my passport is still there. Corporal Kennedy informs us that the Saddam Husseins have taken some cash from his wallet – presumably to cover the cost of our Turkish bath.

'That fuckin' only cost three dollars. One dollar each,' exclaims Corporal Kennedy. 'A fuckin' bargain in any man's language.' Animal is uncharacteristically silent all the way to the hotel.

That night we go to the Syrian version of Tamangos thanks to Corporal Kennedy's 'exclusive' contacts within the Damascus entertainment and night club industries. The night club is in a dingy basement and is packed to the rafters with French speaking Damascus socialites. There is a Russian band playing electric polkas on the stage. Animal challenges them to a musical duel. He outplays them on the mandolin. We get free drink. The musical duelling continues apace. I then stagger on to the stage and grab the 48 bass accordion from the Russians. Corporal Kennedy jumps up and pushes the bouncers away from me.

I play 'Three Blind Mice' from memory. The entire nightclub falls silent. There is then an enormous cheer. Corporal Kennedy is staring at me with a new found respect. 'You. You are some fuckin' banana. I've never met a bleedin' officer like you before.' Animal belches loudly in my ear. 'Ah, ye still have it.' I remember little else of the evening.

The following morning, exhausted, we drive back across the Syrian panhandle towards the Israeli border. The Syrians wave us through their dilapidated dusty checkpoint. The Israelis on the other side wave us through their shining, state of the art checkpoint and search area. Slowly, reluctantly we make our way to the Lebanese border. The temptation to drive to Tel Aviv, abandon the minibus in the airport and fly home to Dublin is strangely compelling. But, no, it's back to the Lebanon, back to Al Yatun. And back to more patrols. Night and day. Day and Night. Watching the murderous crossfire. Wondering if and when we'll be caught up in it. With just a month to go, the odds seem to be lengthening. Unless of course you consider chaos theory – whereby the odds are irrelevant, and the risk ever-present. And Lebanon is a particularly chaotic place just now. And getting more chaotic. We cross the border at Ros Haniqra as the sun is setting. Corporal Kennedy dumps what remains of his suit in Naqoura. We reclaim our rifles, flak jackets and helmets.

We eventually make it back to Camp Shamrock. We part company with Animal in the transport yard where we hand in the keys of the minibus to the Transport Sergeant. He gives it the once over – as if we were at a car rental return at some major international airport. 'Thanks for using rent-a-wreck,' he intones, 'please consider us again for your future travel plans.' Forlorn in our flak jackets we hitch a lift back to Al Yatun. The weather has grown considerably warmer in our absence. Our return coincides with the arrival of the first heatwave in Irishbatt.

Five days later, the heatwave in the AO leads to extended violent thunderstorms. Again, I'm watching the bolt lightning dancing and arcing of aerials, rooftops and treelines. As the rain runs off our helmets and down through the hatches, soaking everything, I wonder what it would be like to get hit by lightning. To get fried on top of the APC by a freak bolt of lightning. I idly wonder about the inscription on my gravestone. 'Here lies Lieutenant Clonan – struck by lighting in Lebanon. Electrocuted by God in the name of international peace.' At least Hizbullah and the Israelis aren't firing at each other all night. I've no sooner had that thought than matters take a turn for the worse once more.

After prayers in the Mosques that Friday, Hizbullah commence a cycle of assaults that lead to more gun battles in the villages of Irishbatt and on the slopes of the Israeli compounds. There are several simultaneous gun battles raging throughout our area. I'm out on patrol near Majdal Silm when it kicks off. The trick is to get back to the cover of the nearest Irish post – Al Jurn – without getting caught in the crossfire. Or without getting targeted ourselves. By either side.

I notice as we head toward Al Jurn that all of the villages and houses are in complete darkness. The only sounds above the constant rain and thunder is the constant crack and thump of the high velocity firefights breaking out in the villages around us. A sinister staccato chattering – high pitched whining and zinging reports. Just like the cheesy soundtrack to the westerns I used to watch at home in Ballygall Avenue. There is no Morricone soundtrack here though. Just the diesel engines. The clanking of the automatic gearbox as the driver goes from Low to High to get us the fuck out of Dodge. I'm thinking about my family and my girlfriend all the time now. Because it is only a matter of weeks before we get out of this madhouse. To be frank, I'm getting fed up of it all. I'm exhausted.

# Chapter 26

# April

*78 Irishbatt Operations Summary April 1996*
*Shooting Incidents: 752, Firings Close to Irishbatt Positions: 39, Serious*
*Incidents involving armed elements: 65, Air Incursions by Israeli Aircraft: 80*

Unit History, 78 Irishbatt, UNIFIL

The first week of April goes by in a blur. The doubling of patrols by the BMR means that we are on the road for almost eighteen hours a day. In between patrols, I attend more and more meetings with the operations officers in Battalion Headquarters. We grab food when we can. As the heat intensifies, we also drink as much water as possible. With temperatures in the mid-thirties, wearing full combats, flak jacket, webbing and a helmet, one sweats continuously. If you don't drink water, if you don't rehydrate constantly, you cannot concentrate. You go a bit fuzzy. Like walking underwater, and you can't do your job. The medics call it the 'GI blues'.

During the latest April attacks by Hizbullah, Operations inform us that seven Israeli soldiers have been killed and sixteen have been seriously injured in the UNIFIL Area of Operations. In retaliation, the Israelis have only managed to kill one Hizbullah fighter. This represents a worrying reversal of combat outcomes for the Israelis. Up to now, Hizbullah attacks on the Israeli firebases have been suicide missions. In what is known euphemistically by the military as the 'exchange ratio', Hizbullah – until now it seems – would lose around seven or eight fighters for every one Israeli killed in action. Over March and April of 1996, that exchange ratio is completely reversed, with Hizbullah killing seven Israelis and seriously wounding sixteen others. This bitter reversal of fortunes is happening during our deployment. The ever-increasing exchanges of fire between the Israelis and Hizbullah and the consequent increase in fatalities is taking place as we double our patrols between the warring parties. I am developing a deep feeling of foreboding. Everything about the operations and intelligence scenario suggests the Israelis will mount a massive retaliation. All we can do is wait. Follow our orders. Show solidarity with the Lebanese civilians amongst whom we patrol. As we check our flak jackets and helmets and think of the mutilated bodies we have evacuated from the villages, wadis and olive groves – the implications and risks of 'flying the flag' are clear to us.

Still, not one of the troops hesitates. No one expresses misgivings. Everyone takes their turn to go on patrol. I am proud of the BMR – proud of the Gunners and Troopers under my command. They are fully aware of the danger to ourselves in patrolling and evacuating the dead and injured. And when the firing starts, the driver's intimate knowledge of the terrain helps us to find dead ground. A mad dash for cover. An adrenaline-fuelled sprint to safety. 'Rushin' Roulette' we call it.

In this deteriorating environment and without exception, troops all over Irishbatt's AO – from the infantry stuck in their posts, to the ordnance, medics and engineering teams in Headquarters – give tirelessly and unflinchingly of themselves. The more shit that hits the fan, the more they rise to each and every occasion. I am proud to be an Irish army officer in all of this mayhem. Proud to serve with these Irish troops whose nerves are stretched to breaking point. The troops use black humour to deal with the stress, the fear, the upset, the grief, the rage and the exhaustion. Throughout all of this, at the back of my mind, I am dismayed – and troubled – that the Irish people, through no fault of their own, are largely unaware of what is going on. Unaware of the sacrifices being made in their name.

With the constant patrolling and the ever-changing and challenging situations we encounter, the BMR have gelled into a finely tuned team. We are all jumpy, but there have been no trigger-happy incidents. No breaks in discipline. Everyone follows orders to the letter. As peacekeepers, there is a tension in being armed 24/7 in such a volatile, unpredictable situation. Self discipline and fire-control is vital. Since the beginning of the deployment, I've insisted on inspecting weapons daily, checking ammunition belts and all of the other ordnance in the Sisus. This was initially greeted with some grumbling and complaint. But, by April, this has become second nature. All of the weapons are perfectly maintained. The ammunition belts are clean, looped properly and free of excess oil and dirt. 'We must have the shiniest, cleanest weapons in the entire Middle East,' observes Sergeant Bracken.

And, it is almost a contradiction in terms. We are armed to the teeth, but we rarely open fire. The Irish have a good record in this regard – preferring to remain part of the solution in Lebanon. Endeavoring at all times to avoid becoming a part of the problem by getting sucked into random fire-fights. There is much provocation. Both the Israelis and Hizbullah constantly test our mental and psychological nerve. Under international law and our UN mandate however, our weapons are for self defence only. We are permitted to use 'minimum force' only, in a very narrow range of circumstances. This calls for strong self control. It requires a high level of discipline and self-restraint not to open fire in some circumstances – to let fly – at something, anything. As an officer,

I'm ultimately responsible for the lives of those who serve with me. I must ensure that we don't get involved in an exchange of fire that leads to fatalities – amongst ourselves or the warring parties. Or, by way of collateral damage, among the civilian population.

It is a tough balancing act. For inevitably, there will be circumstances where it will be essential to open fire in order to stay alive and bring everyone home in one piece. I hope I give the right order if such a split decision must be made. Those involved in the after-action reports and subsequent enquiries will have weeks, months and years to reach a verdict on a split second judgement call. I sometimes wonder at the psychological impact of this restraint in the face of constant provocation.

Everyone's nerves are frayed. So, we keep busy. Making sure that the radios are all serviceable for example. Monitoring the company and battalion tactical net has become second nature, a compulsive, obsessive behaviour with everyone in the BMR – almost like a displacement activity.

On the first weekend of April, I meet Sergeant Fuckin-Fuck outside the Operations room in Al Yatun. He is heading up to the roof with a mug of tea. He has been quieter of late. Subdued. I ask him if he is looking forward to going home. 'Me allowances will pay for me daughter to go to college,' is all he says to me. Later that night, Sergeant Fuckin-Fuck goes into the ammunition store to do an ordnance check. He locks himself inside. He sits down on the plastic bucket seat facing the ammunition trays and kicks the keys out through the gap beneath the door. He takes off his flak jacket and drapes it over his head. He takes his Steyr rifle and cocks it. With the round chambered, he places the muzzle between his teeth. Pointing straight up, through the roof of his mouth. He grips the rifle between his knees and reaches down. He takes up first pressure on the trigger. Then squeezes.

We hear the muffled report from the Operations room. The BS finds the keys on the ground. We open the door. Sergeant Fuckin-Fuck's body is lying slumped forward. Blood, bits of his skull and brain matter have exploded out of the sides of his flak jacket. The material creates an unusual spray pattern across the walls and ammunition trays. No more Sergeant Fuckin-Fuck.

We have no time to come to terms with his death. The following night, Hizbullah launch their first attack of April. Just before 11 PM, they launch a massed coordinated attack on the Cuckoos Nest. DFF 13 returns fire. Before midnight, the entire Area of Operations is alight with tracer fire criss-crossing the wadis. The artillery batteries at Gate 12 and Gate 14 Alpha open fire. Irish voices flood the radio net reporting impacts, near misses and firings close from all over Irishbatt. The night patrol has been caught out in the open again and the BMR are careering – once more – up the dirt road from Brashit towards a junction leading to Tibnine and the relative safety Al Yatun. The lads are completely silent. The usual cursing and banter in the Sisu has been replaced with silence – save for the growing volume of radio traffic. As the vehicles roar through Tibnine, there is a deafening thunderclap overhead. The Sisu shudders and slews to one side. The internal lights go out, flicker and blink and then fail altogether. The driver is revving the engine and frantically working the gearbox. Eventually the Sisu lurches forward and gains momentum once more for Al Yatun. When the Sisus clatter across the cattle grid at 6-40 everyone heaves a collective sigh of relief. The left hand side of the Sisu has been raked by shrapnel. Two of the massive tyres are shredded. White paint and part of the UN lettering on the side of the armour have been sandblasted off the vehicle by the shrapnel.

The fitter sergeant and his crew are waiting. By morning the tyres have been replaced. The armour resprayed. It is a sobering experience for all of us. Sergeant Bracken puts an Advent calendar up on the inside of the metal hatch of the Sisu. He changes the dates from December to April. 'We'll have a countdown to getting out of here,' he says. The guys look at the calendar. 'Two weeks to go to the first rotation,' intones Sergeant Bracken. As he heads back to his billet with his backpack and his rifle, he calls out to me in the darkness, 'Wake me up in fourteen days.'

The following morning, 9 April, we are awoken by a series of Katyusha missile attacks on Israel from with Irishbatt's Area of Operations. Hizbullah are following up on their attacks on the compounds with this serious escalation in hostilities. Defying international law and the Geneva Conventions, Hizbullah are now firing salvo after salvo of Katyusha missiles point blank into Israel. They are firing indiscriminately at Israeli towns and villages such as Kiryat Shmona, Rihaniya, Meron and Eilon. Targeting civilians in their homes; children in their beds. In the coming days Hizbullah will seriously injure sixty-two innocent Israeli civilians in these malicious attacks. Tens of thousands of innocent civilians in Northern Israel will be forced to spend days and weeks in bomb shelters as a result.

Israel eventually responds with the expected retaliation and saturates the Area of Operations with artillery fire and air strikes. Much of the retaliatory fire falls around our positions. I'm glad I'm not on patrol as the bombardment commences. We hunker down in 6-40 and fire red flares as the rounds impact around us. The radios relay the hundreds of artillery and air strikes back to Battalion Headquarters. Such is the volume of radio traffic that the Operations staff impose radio silence on all but the most urgent requests for assistance.

On the morning of 12 April, the Israeli-sponsored 'Voice of the South' radio station announces that Israel will 'Avenge Hizbullah rocket attacks on Northern Israel.' An Israeli military statement goes on to say that 'The residents of Brashit, Shaqra, Majdal Silm, Safad, Jumay Jumay, Tibnine and Haddathah have four hours to leave their homes before the Israeli Army shells them'. This sinister message is broadcast repeatedly over the next hour or so. Within Irishbatt, chaos ensues. Thousands of villagers flood the dirt roads and tracks attempting to flee the area. They pass through our checkpoints en masse. Men, women and children are packed into cars, vans and trucks of all descriptions. Tractors and trailers piled high with people pass through the checkpoints. Men, women and children cling to whatever they can. Clinging for dear life. They bring whatever meagre possessions they can carry. I see one elderly couple lying on a mattress tied to the roof of a car. Covered by a tattered duvet and holding one another tightly, their extended family crammed into the ancient battered Mercedes below.

Those that cannot drive or hitch a lift walk through the checkpoints. It is a full scale exodus on a biblical scale. Many of those on foot are the elderly or infirm with no adult children to help them flee. In one particularly distressing scene, an elderly couple attempt to encourage and coax their adult child with Down Syndrome up the road. He is screaming in terror and distress, tears streaming down his cheeks. When the A Company troops try to help this family group, he recoils in horror and shrieks even louder. Terrified by the uniforms.

Mothers nursing babies are also among the throng. As the Israeli deadline approaches, the women divert from the road and begin to push their way into our position at Al Yatun. We are in danger of being over-run by civilian refugees. The quartermasters are running around handing out ration packs to the troops. They in turn are handing them to the women and children. Soon, the entire post is lined up at the perimeter fence, handing out precious bottles of water, milk, yoghurt, dollars. Anything and everything. Toys and teddy bears intended for Irish children in Dublin, Cork, Mullingar and Kildare are pushed through the wire into the hands of small terrified children who have been forced to evacuate. Small comfort.

I am at the checkpoint with the NCOs watching the exodus. Among the crowd I see a teenage boy in a wheelchair. He is desperately trying to keep up with the group but is clearly foundering in the crush.

Radio silence is still being imposed on our tactical nets due to the sheer volume of traffic. This apocalyptic event is unfolding so rapidly, we are struggling to keep pace with matters. We learn that the Israeli government is calling this retaliation 'Operation Grapes of Wrath'. The punitive action has been personally approved of by the Israeli Prime Minister, Shimon Peres, as a collective punishment for the people of Lebanon. To teach them that support for Hizbullah and its criminal attacks on Israel will 'cost Lebanon dearly'. As we watch the growing number of refugees flee the villages, the Israeli military launch airstrikes all over Lebanon. From the Bekaa Valley, to Beirut and all along the coast road from Sidon down to Tyre. All hell has broken loose. The massive power stations at Jumhour and Bsaleem outside Beirut are destroyed in Israeli air strikes. The lights go off all over Lebanon. Pandemonium reigns.

By that afternoon on the 12th, the Israelis have moved significant artillery and air assets north to the border with Lebanon. There is an eerie calm amid the growing storm. Panic begins to kick in as the deadline for all-out mayhem approaches. As I drive out of the gate of Al Yatun to attend another briefing in Camp Shamrock, a young woman surges forward and reaches up to me with her infant. She pleads with me to take her baby to safety. Sergeant Bracken is taking this in and calls over to me from the other hatch. In the moment it takes him to shout, 'Whatever you do, don't take the baby,' the young woman, panic stricken, gently tosses the baby into my arms. The driver stands on the brakes.

Miraculously, at that moment, the Battalion Commander comes over the Motorola net and orders all of Irishbatt's positions to open our gates to the refugees. With a huge sigh of relief, we open the gates of 6-40 and the Lebanese fall into our arms. Mother is re-united with baby. It is an experience that will return to haunt me in future years. In ways that I cannot yet understand. Within minutes, Al Yatun – with a population of around a hundred Irish troops – now has an additional population of approximately three hundred men, women and children.

The men congregate together and smoke. The women tend to the elderly and the sick, along with the children. I see the wheelchair boy being carried up the steps of the canteen by two troops from A Company. He has been given a can of Coke. All three are laughing. Some shared joke. I hear Mad Bastard tell the boy, 'This is the best bleedin' bar in South Lebanon.'

Within minutes, the Israeli bombardment begins. Hafif wails, 'Jazes, Jazes, Jazes,' in a flat Dublin accent. At the same time, the BMR gets the order to patrol the now deserted villages. The duty officer at Battalion Headquarters tells me that it is imperative that we maintain a presence in the villages. To physically signal the presence of the UN. To prevent the further 'ethnic cleansing' of innocent Lebanese civilians from their homes.

I warn BS Joyce that we may be on patrol for an indefinite period of time, with no certain prospect of returning to Al Yatun. I order him to instruct the troops to gather up whatever ration packs, water and batteries they can find in the precious few minutes left to us before we depart Al Yatun.

I run to my billet, pushing my way through the civilian refugees. I grab two or three litre bottles of water. I take a fleeting glance at the letters home that I had intended to post. Too late for that now. As I head back out to the Sisu, I check for the St Christopher medal that my Mum – despite my objections – had sewn in to the hem of my combat jacket. I wonder what my parents are doing at that moment. Hanging out the washing in our garden in Ballygall Avenue maybe. I wondered what my girlfriend is doing. Probably on her way to or from work. Stuck in rush hour traffic. I say a quick prayer for them all. It never occurs to me to pray for myself. But then, I have BS Begley, Sergeant Bracken and Corporal Kennedy on my side. What can possibly go wrong?

As we roll out the gate, the Israelis declare the entire Area of Operations a 'Free Fire Zone'. Our forlorn hope is that the white paint on our vehicles and blue UN flags will offer us some protection. We know from experience that the protection offered by our armour is limited. Off the coast, the Israeli Navy enforce a naval blockade of Tyre, Sidon and Beirut. The entire country of Lebanon is held in a stranglehold. We hear on the radio that all traffic on the coastal highway is being fired on. As we head down the potholed track into a deteriorating operational environment I hear Corporal Kennedy clearing his throat on my headphones. 'Where's me bleedin' camera? I want to get some photos of them Israeli Helicopters.' I sincerely hope we don't get the photo opportunities he craves.

# Chapter 27

# Grapes of Wrath

*C'mon now. Fuck it. C'mon now. C'mon*

As we drive through the throng of refugees fleeing the area we get official confirmation over the radio that the Israelis have commenced shelling the villages of Shaqra, Majdal Silm and Brashit. For the Israelis, H Hour has arrived. Operation Grapes of Wrath is underway. There is a report of a direct hit on a civilian car on the outskirts of Brashit. We are not far from Al Jurn when we get this message and we divert to the scene.

About 1km from Brashit there is a car lying on its side across the roadway. A woman approaches us waving what looks like a white pillow case. It is heavily bloodstained and there is blood running down her face from under her headscarf. We pull up and dismount. Corporal Kennedy runs past her to the car which is on fire. He has taken one of the fire extinguishers from the Sisu with him. Sergeant Bracken is talking to the woman in soothing tones. Trying to get her to calm down. He leads her to the back doors of the Sisu and is offering her water. She is incoherent and is jabbing her finger towards the car on the road. Speaking Arabic too quickly for us to make any sense of the words.

I hear the whoosh of the fire extinguisher as Corporal Kennedy puts out the flames that are flickering around the doorframe on the passenger side. He is joined by two of the Gunners who start pulling the door open. There is a boy inside. We later learn that he is fourteen years old. The car is filled to the ceiling with family belongings. Bed linen, clothes. Water. Things that the family had grabbed at the last minute. The boy's school-books are also strewn around the car. They pull him out gently. He is limp. His eyes are open. The armoured ambulance arrives on the scene and the medics from Battalion Headquarters sprint towards the car.

Corporal Kennedy is cursing now as the paramedics start CPR on the boy. 'C'mon now. Fuck it. C'mon now. C'mon.' But it is too late. We inform operations about the casualty on the Motorola. The Operations staff tell me that the Israelis are firing on the Red Crescent ambulances in Tibnine. We'll have to bring the boy in ourselves.

We find the boy's father standing under a tree a short distance away. He has a head injury and is highly agitated. He struggles with us as we shepherd him back to the Sisus. Sergeant Bracken and Corporal Kennedy have put the boy on some of the bed linen in the footwell of the armoured ambulance. The medics have closed the boy's eyes and it is as though he is sleeping on the floor. In a split second I take in his Nike trainers. And his stonewashed jeans. I am conscious of the love and care invested in this boy. Now broken and lifeless in the dirty footwell of the APC.

Sergeant Bracken and the boy's mother are in the rear Sisu now. The mother is sobbing. The father is still agitated and is calling out the boy's name. The gunners push the car off the roadway. We confirm our actions on the Motorola and signal our intention to return to Tibnine with the family. It is a silent journey. Seems to take forever. I cannot bring myself to look at the armoured ambulance. And the thoughts of the dead boy down below in its green-lit interior.

The shelling is relentless despite the mounting toll of Lebanese casualties. So far, no Hizbullah fighters have fallen victim to the bombardment. Just villagers trying to flee. Caught in the open. Others are trapped in their homes. Left behind. Abandoned to their fate. Many of the villages have elderly people who are too old, too sick to leave. In some cases, young mothers breastfeeding infants have been unable to escape. Many have husbands who are stranded in Tyre, Sidon or Beirut. As they become dehydrated, they are unable to feed their babies. In these circumstances, desperate for drinking water, these women take to the roads and tracks in search of help. Sometimes with fatal consequences. As the following days go by, the BMR is increasingly tasked with evacuating the dead and injured from dozens of villages where families have found themselves trapped by the bombardment. We also bring fresh water and other humanitarian aid to those still living who remain trapped. We evacuate those who wish to leave. Many are too sick, frightened or bewildered to leave with us.

The weekend is a continuous unending loop of constant patrolling through the bombardment. We deliver aid where we can. We provide escorts to the Red Crescent evacuating the dead and injured from houses that have received direct hits. In Shaqra, we escort Engineers and Medics from Camp Shamrock as they dig bodies out of a row of houses that have been destroyed by shellfire. They work frantically in the hope of digging out survivors. They use diesel generators to power massive consaws – cutting through twisted metal supports and concrete to uncover the dead. Family groups. Children and parents alike, crushed, burned, dismembered by the shelling. Above ground and at the edges of the destroyed houses there is the detritus of family life. A child's tricycle. Family photographs. Bits of delph and cutlery. Thrown up in the high tide of high explosives.

The engineers lift the bodies out one by one. Some of the bundles are pitifully small. The engineers and medics are drawn from units all over Ireland. There is a mix of Dublin, Donegal and Midland accents as they gently place the bodies in the Red Crescent ambulances or into the footwells of the Sisus. Some of the lads are praying. Some of them are wiping away tears of rage and frustration. And then, we hear the distant thump thump thump of more artillery headed our way. Under incoming fire, the engineers are forced to abandon the rescue and recovery effort. Everyone is angered by this. But we are too busy to stop, reflect or discuss any of it. We know that our headquarters is reporting each and every incident through UNIFIL Headquarters to the UN in New York. We can only hope that the international community are listening to us and to our calls for a cease fire. On the ground, Hizbullah are not interested in a cessation of hostilities. They continue to launch salvo after salvo of Katyusha rockets into Israeli territory. And Israel responds by continuing the collective punishment. The cycle of violence continues with the Irish in the eye of the storm.

By Monday, 15 April, the number of Lebanese refugees sheltering in Al Yatun has risen to 350. Because of the naval blockade and the constant shelling, the Battalion is running low on water, fuel and fresh food. We have fallen back on our reserves of ration packs. Water is strictly rationed. It is for drinking only. The Israeli Air Force are constantly criss-crossing our AO. The endless series of sonic booms – we think at times, designed simply to intimidate us and terrorise the civilian population – has destroyed all of our cisterns and water butts. There is no water to flush toilets. Nor is there water to wash or shower. The septic tanks are overflowing with the crush of humanity on the base. The place stinks to high heaven of human shit. The villages stink of shit and decaying flesh. Under the rubble, unattended bodies are decomposing in the heat. We estimate that at least sixty to seventy bodies of innocent civilians are lying unrecovered in the villages around Al Yatun and Tibnine. Distressed live-stock and dead animals add to the harrowing scene.

Despite this, the refugees in Al Yatun are cheerful. The troops – pre-dictably – play with the kids and try to console them. The refugees look to us for reassurance every time a shell impacts our position. In the after-noon of Monday, 15 April, two Israeli Helicopter Gunships rake Al Yatun, Haris and neighbouring Haddathah with machine gun and rocket fire. The refugees are terrified. At the same time, to the north of our posi-tion, two Israeli jets attack the village of As Sultaniyah. A cry of alarm rises up from the refugees in Al Yatun when they observe the water tower in As Sultaniyah receive a direct hit from a 500lb bomb. It is obliterated in one strike. The ground shakes. We consider the damage a direct hit would do on the press of humanity huddled in Al Yatun for safety. But, surely the Israelis will not fire directly on a UN position? This thought gives us some comfort.

Later, on that Monday evening, the BMR are tasked with recovering bodies from the road between Al Yatun and Qana. We are ordered to provide an escort for the Red Crescent ambulance from Tibnine hospi-tal. The Red Crescent paramedics are in fear of their lives as they have been repeatedly fired upon. We hope that our presence will deter either side from interfering with them.

# Chapter 28

# Collateral Damage

*It's just a bad day at the office*

I am in the back hatch of the rear Sisu as we head towards the village of Qana. Kfar Qana is where, as Psycho puts it, 'Jesus, allegedly, turned the water into wine.' As we approach Qana the streets of the small villages en route are deserted, the houses shuttered. The footpaths and alleyways are strewn with fallen masonry which has been blasted off the exterior walls by shrapnel and machine gun fire. Wires hang in looms over the road as many of the concrete telegraph poles have been shattered and broken by the artillery and air strikes. We scan the road carefully for low hanging wires and move slowly. None of us wants to be decapitated by a stray loop of low hanging wire. We keep waving at the Red Crescent ambulance. It is an ancient Citroen, low to the ground. Its suspension a distant memory. No doubt victim to the potholed roads and tracks. Giving the driver the thumbs up for confidence. His hands grip the steering wheel and he keeps looking up, scanning the skyline for Israeli helicopters.

We continue along the road towards the boundary of Irishbatt. As we round a bend we see the remains of a car on the road. All that is left of the car – a silver blue Mercedes – is the engine block. It has part-melted into the road surface. The burnt black metal congealed in tarmac. The driver, somehow, is still intact. Well, half of him is. Most of the upper body, and his head – minus the jaw which has been blown away – is lying in the road. Arms at silly angles. And his upper teeth – an image that remains with me – are stuck in the melting tarmac next to the engine block. It is an impossible arrangement.

The car has been struck by a Tow missile fired from an Israeli helicopter earlier in the afternoon. Bits of the Mercedes are strewn over the olive grove next to the road. The bonnet hangs from an olive tree some fifty metres away. Corporal Kennedy eyes me with malicious curiosity. 'Are ye all right?' he asks me mischievously. His sing-song Dublin accent – the accent of my childhood in Finglas has a playful lilt to it. He has obviously recovered from the death of the fourteen-year-old boy in Brashit. This is different I suppose, the victim is an adult. We also suspect that he is Hizbullah. Corporal Kennedy whistles as he crouches over the body. 'That's his last meal – eating the fuckin' road by the looks of it.' The Motorola hisses and squawks into life. 'Hello 42 Alpha, this is Zero, Message, Over. For your information and necessary action, Gate 14 Alpha has commenced firing into your grid position. Over.' I tell Zero over the Motorola that we are removing the 'casualty' to Tibnine Hospital. 'Roger, Out' is the crackled reply.

So, we watch as the Red Crescent guys scrape him off the road. They carefully pry the teeth free from the tarmac and slide the remains into a body bag. Corporal Kennedy is sweating profusely. Once the whole sorry, sordid affair is over, he makes eye contact as we heave ourselves, weapons, and flak jackets back into the Sisu. He thrusts his face close to mine. He whispers, fiercely, urgently. 'Lighten up for fuck's sake. It's just a bad day at the office.' We laugh all the way back to Tibnine.

All through that Monday night, the Israelis continue their attacks across the AO. Thousands of houses are destroyed in artillery and air strikes. Tracer shells rip through the night blackness. Mortars continuously thumping as they are launched from the Israeli firebases on the ridgeline opposite us. We sense the long lazy arc of their steep trajectory and tense up as the 120mm mortars crash heavily into the villages and tracks around us. Tanks shells – with that signature slapping sound you get with flat trajectories – slam into buildings and outhouses throughout the night. The ground vibrates constantly. Night blurs into day.

At first light on Tuesday, 16 April, the BMR are again requested to assist in the removal of dead and injured civilians from the little village of Jumay Jumay. There is unexploded ordnance strewn throughout Jumay Jumay and we liaise with the Ordnance Officer from Battalion Headquarters. The Ordnance detachment give us the thumbs up and we proceed cautiously into the village. A group of elderly stragglers – stranded in the mostly deserted village – emerge blinking into the morning light. They are agitated and upset and are pointing and gesticulating at a badly damaged house at the end of the narrow street. We dismount and move towards the building.

BS Begley is the first to enter the house. Its door is still standing though hanging on its hinges. He pushes past it and disappears inside. He is followed by Sergeant Bracken. I'm on the back hatch checking in with Battalion Headquarters when Sergeant Bracken backs out of the doorway. He is carrying the body of a small boy. The boy is wearing a little Kermit the Frog T-shirt. Covered in dust, Kermit still waves jauntily. But the small boy is stiff with rigor mortis. I remember him from our day at Finnbatt range. The BS follows Sergeant Bracken carrying the body of the older boy.

BS Begley calls out to us as they lay the bodies down gently on the ground. 'There's a whole family in here. Not a mark on them.' The Red Crescent arrive from Tibnine and one by one the bodies are brought out.

All four children, including the little girl that we fed on our day in Finnbatt range are laid out. The little girl lies in among her brothers. The entire family is removed to the morgue in Tibnine Hospital.

When we eventually get back to Al Yatun the mayhem continues. Commandant McManus of A Company is holding a conference among his infantry officers in the Operations room. I notice how tired he looks. His face lined and grey. He is covered in a fine white dust. So is everybody. Everyone is exhausted. Some of the platoon commanders in A Company are classmates of mine from the Cadet School. I don't envy their confinement to the hilltop posts and checkpoints in the villages. Some of the A Company posts are situated right next to the Israeli compounds. Despite the element of risk – I'm happier to be free and mobile, patrolling through the entirety of the area of operations. I have a chance to go to my billet to change my combats which are filthy and soaked in sweat. I catch a glimpse of myself in the little shaving mirror at the end of the bed. I see myself reflected. Covered in the same dust as Mac and the infantry officers. I'd give anything to lie down on the bed. Even just for a few moments.

Mac tells us that the international media are converging on Beirut and are trying to get south to cover what is now – at last – becoming an international news story. The media are managing to get to Beirut via Damascus and Turkey but cannot get south along the coast road because the Israelis have declared the coastal highway a free fire zone and are firing on all vehicles travelling north or south. A news crew from the UK's ITN has managed to get south of the Litani. The BMR is tasked to escort them into the AO.

The following day we meet the ITN guys. Three of them, presenter, cameraman and sound operator. Their reporter is Alex Thompson who will later become Channel Four's chief news reporter. They are subdued and go about their work quietly and efficiently. We bring them out to Jumay Jumay so that they can film the recovery of bodies there. We then bring them to Shaqra to witness a similar operation there with the Battalion's information officer. I'm standing up on the back hatch watching them film and do their pieces to camera when we get word of a shell warning for the area. We reluctantly withdraw to Tibnine where they film large numbers of wounded being treated by local medical staff. It is reassuring to know that at last the world community will hear of what is being perpetrated here by Hizbullah on one side – and the IDF on the other.

We leave the Channel Four crew in Tibnine and are ordered back to Shaqra to bring fresh water, medicine and food to the civilians still stranded there. We take one of the battalion's interpreters with us to try and persuade some of the locals to evacuate back to Al Yatun or any of the Irish UN positions in the area. The interpreter chain smokes as we bump and rattle back up the tracks to Shaqra. The village is deserted. There is fallen masonry all over the footpaths. The metal shutters of various shopfronts and small businesses are torn up with shrapnel. Some are peeled back at awkward angles reflecting the blast patterns of direct hits from Israeli artillery and rocket fire.

We rev the engines as we turn around at the village water hole and move slowly back through the village. Pausing under some shredded awnings, I ask the driver to sound the klaxon a few times. Eventually, some elderly people appear from the shadows and the darkened interior of the partially destroyed houses. We form a human chain and start passing water and ration packs into their basements and cellars. The interpreter is nowhere to be seen. I wander back to the Sisu and find him sitting in the rear smoking his cigarettes. I ask him to come out and talk to the locals for us. He refuses point blank. 'It is not my job. Too fucking dangerous. Just hurry up and get out of here.' I cannot believe my ears. The anger and frustration of the last few days and weeks wells up inside me.

I tell him to get out and help us ferry the water to the elderly. To help his neighbours. He refuses once more. 'They are not my fucking neighbours. I am not from Shaqra.'

I grab him by the lapels and pull him out through the rear doors. I push him out past the rear doors and into the nearest doorway. 'You can smoke here and watch us then. Smoke as much as you fucking like. Smoke your fucking brains out.' He tells me that I will be in big trouble with the senior officers back in Camp Shamrock.

The last thing I hear him say is, 'I am interpreter. It is not my job to lift fucking bottles.'

On the way back to Tibnine, the interpreter glowers at me from inside the APC. But he says nothing and I'm glad he doesn't provoke me. When we get into Shamrock to refuel, he slinks away without a word.

BS Begley asks me to sign for the fuel. I tell him about the interpreter. I express my disbelief that we have come all the way from Ireland to help and that he, a local, refuses to assist his elderly neighbours in Shaqra. BS Begley looks at me and says in a low voice so that he cannot be overheard. 'Did you not notice how frightened he was. He was shitting himself all the way out to Shaqra. He's desperate to save face. He'd say black was white to stay in the Sisu.' I think about this. For a split second I feel guilty. But I don't have time to reflect. And I think, 'Fuck him. Fuck the lot of them.' Over the following seventy-two hours, over 25,000 Israeli artillery shells rain down on us. It is impossible to think straight let alone wrestle with one's conscience. Or to try and second guess anyone else.

Throughout this time, the Irish troops perform miracles. Up in Al Yatun, the cooks perform the miracle of the loaves and the fishes. They feed the troops and all 350 refugees while under constant fire. At one point, I encounter Pops – the cook sergeant – in a state of near exhaustion outside the cookhouse. He is lying half asleep next to piles of ration packs. Alarmingly, he is also wearing nothing but his green army-issue Y-fronts. I ask him if he is OK. He looks up at me blinking in the sunlight. 'I'm trying to get a fucking tan here, Sir. Would you mind stepping back a bit? We've only got two weeks to go. I'm not going home as white as a fucking milk bottle.' I leave him to it.

The medics are working steadily through the family groups of refugees. Examining them, treating minor ailments. Trying to find out what medication is required by the elderly. The kids get to watch *The Lion King* in the canteen. Over and over again. 'Hakuna Matata' becomes the watchword once more. In the middle of all of this, Psycho announces from the Operations room. '*Éist le Seo*. Telephone Call from Ireland for Lieutenant Clonan. Lieutenant Clonan. Yer Da's on the phone.' I break into a sprint and take the handset from Psycho. Mac looks up from his O group where he and a group of infantry officers and NCOs are poring over some maps. He winks at me.

I take the phone. Over the distance of thousands of miles and the crackling line, I hear my father's distant and disembodied voice. 'Thomas. Are you all right? It said on the news that a bomb went off on the border between Israel and Lebanon.' I convince him that I'm fine. I tell him that it is quiet where we are and not to worry. 'That's what I thought all right. Don't frighten your mother. She's worried sick. Here, I'll put her on.' My mother comes on the phone. In the crowded operations room, against the background of the crump and wallop of the ongoing Israeli barrage, she asks me if I'm OK. Her voice sounds a long way off. She tells me that she'll say a decade of the rosary for me. She tells me to wrap up well during the night-time as this is the time of year when you'd get a chill. Then the line goes dead.

Psycho announces that the Padre is on the base. Fr Ryan leads a short service of commemoration for Sergeant Fuckin-Fuck in the canteen. About fifty curious Lebanese refugees attend the service. Fr Ryan quips that the Sergeant would have been proud of the big turn out. It is one of the few laughs we get that week. The padre chats to Shia holy men among the crowd. They pray together. For the Irish. For the Lebanese. For peace.

# Chapter 29

# Qana

*It should not be hidden from you that the people of Islam had suffered from aggression, iniquity and injustice imposed on them by the Zionist-Crusaders [...] The horrifying pictures of the massacre of Qana, in Lebanon are still fresh in our memory. All of this [...] a clear conspiracy between the USA and its allies and under the cover of the iniquitous United Nations*

Fatwa or declaration of war issued by Osama bin Laden and Al Qaeda on the United States after the Qana Massacre, Lebanon, April 1996

On Wednesday night we continue our patrols through the ongoing nocturnal firefights and tracer fire. To 'fly the flag'. White Phosphorous shells detonate continuously overhead, illuminating the shattered land-scape. It gives the AO an other-worldly appearance. We meander through the tracks and villages, constantly seeking dead ground and cover. We monitor the skyline and watch the unending exchanges of hostile fire. We listen to the radio nets for any hint of imminent or proximate offensive activity or threat.

Meanwhile, far away in New York – lunchtime Eastern Standard Time – negotiations have begun at the UN. The US have managed to broker peace talks between the Syrians, Lebanese and Israelis. There is hope for a ceasefire. Shimon Peres however, is facing an election in Israel. For the moment, he is keen to continue to play the role of strong man for all it is worth. Hizbullah are anxious to continue the war also. They remain fanatical in their hatred of Israel and are making great political capital on the basis of the suffering – imposed by Operation Grapes of Wrath – on innocent Lebanese citizens. For its part, Syria is happy to continue a war of attrition against Israel by way of a proxy conflict in Lebanon.

The collective punishment that is Grapes of Wrath is radicalizing the Lebanese and driving them into the arms of Hizbullah. Others in the Middle East – from Iran to Egypt – are also watching with interest. They publicly sympathise with the plight of the Lebanese. In private, they rejoice in Israel's discomfort. With this schadenfreude however, there is a growing wariness on the part of all interested parties – particularly in Sunni dominated countries – of Hizbullah's growing military prowess and the rise of fundamentalist Islam in the Middle East.

Ops call me on the Motorola at about 3 AM. They tell me that a convoy of Israeli armour has been seen moving towards Irish position 21 and 21 Alpha near Bayt Yahun. I am ordered to take the Sisus up to Bayt Yahun in order to block the road and reinforce the Irish posts. I relay the instructions over the internal net in the Sisus. No one says a word. The mood is uncharacteristically sombre. There are no wisecracks. Our black humour has deserted us momentarily. The driver comes back to me on the net and discusses different routes to Bayt Yahun. We agree on the fastest, most direct route.

When we get to the Irish post, it is illuminated by moonlight. No cloud cover whatsoever. The wadi and rocky slopes around us look like a moonscape. The forbidding Israeli compound DFF 20 Alpha – directly in front of us and overlooking us – is in complete darkness. We strain our ears and hear the distinct clattering and squealing of Israeli armour in the distance. The engine sounds suggest they are manoeuvring into one of their defensive positions. There is a lot of revving and shouting.

215

The infantry officer from C Company is a classmate of mine. He comes to the gate of the post grinning. He asks me if we have any fresh food. They've been eating ration packs for a week now and are sick of the oaten AB biscuits and the powdered coffee. They've given all the chicken curries and chocolate to the remaining kids who come foraging and scrounging for food each day. Miraculously, by a fortunate twist of fate, Corporal Kennedy roots around in his backpack and produces a block of cheddar and a slice pan. He explains to us that earlier in the day Pops had taken the last of the bread out of the freezers in Al Yatun when the generators went offline – having run out of diesel. The infantry guys have a toasted sandwich maker. A match made in heaven. When we plug it in, the lights on the post go a little dimmer and the generator hums at a slightly different pitch. But we have toasted cheese sandwiches. My classmate writes us an IOU for the cheese. Black humour restored. 'I'll get you a block of Calvita when we're home, Clonan.' The Israeli engines start up again just over the hill. We wearily return to the Sisus and take up our positions. Fergus shouts up at me – 'Some last supper, Clonan. Toasted cheese specials.'

We wait in the darkness. At first light the Israelis move up to the crest of the hill and take up positions along the ridge line. They examine us from that short distance with binoculars. They wave and whistle at us from time to time. One of them comes forwards and leaves a cardboard box of milk and yoghurts on the road. One of the infantry guys goes up and drags it into the post. We return the gesture and leave a pile of AB Oat biscuits on the road. Unsurprisingly perhaps, the Israelis aren't interested. They remain on the ridgeline. The main armament on the Merkava tanks occasionally traverse and bead in on us. I think this is just to intimidate. I hope. There is a rumour that the Israelis are going to advance through our positions and re-take south Lebanon as far north of the Litani. To push Hizbullah and their missiles out of range of Israeli territory. We're supposed to stop them. Me, and Corporal Kennedy fortified by toasted cheese sandwiches. I get acid reflux.

As the sun comes up and the morning wears on there is a lot of firing in the B Company area south east of our position. Eventually, we get the order to move down to Haddathah and await instructions there. As we move off, I wave at Fergus through the perimeter fence. He thanks us again for the cheese and says that it is the only useful thing he's ever seen an artillery officer do. As we disappear down the track, Corporal Kennedy breaks the tension. He belches loudly and shouts out to the Israelis above us. They are well beyond earshot. 'Thanks for the milk. And another sleepless night in South Lebanon. Fuck you very much.'

We wait in Haddathah for further instructions. We wait until after midday. In army parlance, we hurry up and wait. It is hard to stay awake. We take it in turns to walk around the Sisus. We clean weapons. Wipe the thousands of rounds of ammunition clear of oil and dirt. We check and re-check the anti-tank rounds and the mortars we have onboard. Anything to stay awake. It is very hot. We have a limited supply of water and I am nursing my bottle of warm water. The Mingy Men have fled to Beirut. There isn't a cold drink to be had anywhere. Then the radio comes into life. Ops call me up on the Motorola. A convoy of media have arrived at Al Yatun. We are to return to 6-40 and make ready to escort the journalists out of the AO towards Tyre. Through Qana.

We get down to Al Yatun. The journalists are walking among the refugees on the post interviewing them about their experiences. Robert Fisk is among them. We are introduced to Fisk. He looks as strained and weary as we do. He is obviously moved by the plight of the refugees. He takes time to talk to everybody. To elicit everyone's opinion. He does so in a quiet, understated way. We are strangely comforted by his presence, confident that the story will now be told. He is an excellent ambassador for journalists – of whom we are very suspicious. Resentful as we are of their freedom of movement and their ability to leave the AO for their air-conditioned hotels and bars on the coast.

One journalist asks me if the UN is a paper tiger. He asks me why we haven't taken the fight to the Israelis. He doesn't ask me anything about Hizbullah. He doesn't ask me my name either. Or where I'm from. He obviously hasn't read anything about the peacekeeping mandate under which we labour. He doesn't ask us anything about the people we've helped. Also, he is wearing tan combat trousers and boots. Along with what looks like a hunting vest – complete with cloth loops for shotgun cartridges. *De rigeur* attire for war correspondents it seems. I know I wouldn't wear anything approximate to a uniform out here. I'm quietly musing if he's likely to get shot by a trigger-happy Israeli or an angry Hizbullah fighter when he interrupts me again. He's asking me what kind of weapons we are carrying when suddenly the radios spring into life.

The initial radio transmissions are garbled. Something about a direct hit on our neighbouring UN position at Qana. It seems the Fijians have had a close call. We know that there are almost 800 civilian refugees crammed into the Fijian post. As more and more reports come in on the net, it becomes clear that the Fijians have taken several direct hits to the post. The first incident reports are suggesting that it is a 'mass casualty' incident.

Within moments, the BMR and Irishbatt's Medical Staff are mobilised to render assistance to the dead and dying in Qana. To bring emergency medical aid and whatever other assistance we can give. We later learn that at approximately 2.08 PM – while we were talking to the journalists in Al Yatun – the Israelis bracketed their artillery fire directly onto the Fijian UN position in Qana. Around thirty-eight high explosive anti-personnel rounds have impacted directly into the crowded post. 155mm artillery shells fired by the Israelis.

As a consequence, 106 men, women and children now lie dead in the post. Their charred, blackened and mutilated remains strewn about the position. A further 116 are seriously wounded. When the Irish arrive at the scene, the Fijians are punch drunk. In shock. The majority of the dead and wounded had been sheltering in one large building with concrete uprights and a roof supported by steel girders. The blast effect of the artillery rounds has literally rendered most of the victims around the concrete posts and roof supports. Human remains and body parts hang from the ceiling and are pooled and intertwined around the floor. It is a charnel house. An abattoir. The shock wave effect of the high explosives has pulped the internal organs of those caught in the attack. Bones are shattered. Bodies blown open. Pink and blue viscera protrude from the bodies of children. Those who were standing are decapitated. Limb separation is another feature of the blast effect of the explosives.

The heat effects are horrific. Many of the bodies are burned beyond recognition. One of the first Irish troops at the scene is met with an elderly woman carrying a decapitated infant. Her grandson. She pleads with him in Arabic to find his head so that he can be buried whole. Someone finds the tiny head. For the first hour or so there is a frantic rush to help the injured and dying. The medical personnel perform miracles and save countless lives. They do so in near silence. Moving among the victims, triaging – separating those who can be helped from the dead and dying. The rest of the troops, with little more than first aid training, move among the injured. They give help where they can, comfort where they cannot. Soldiers from Dublin, Mullingar, Kildare, Cork and Donegal move among the carnage. Whispered accents from all over Ireland soothing the dying.

As some semblance of control is brought to bear on the situation, relays of UN soldiers arrive from all over UNIFIL to assist in the incident. Fresh Irish troops arrive and help to gather together the body parts. They help the Imams and holy men to ready the dead for burial. They help the UN investigators and medical staff to separate the body parts and to log the victims by age and sex. Others use hoses and large yard brushes to sweep and wash away the blood and other matter – all that is left of the victims. At the time of the attack, an Israeli drone is filmed hovering in the vicinity, presumably directing fire onto the UN post.

Initially, the Israelis deny that they have deliberately targeted the post. However, a subsequent UN investigation will conclude that the pattern of the shelling and the circumstantial evidence surrounding the massacre is at variance with Israeli claims of human error in their shelling. The mass killing bears the hallmarks of a premeditated systematic attack on innocent civilians. Not unlike the tactics and strategy employed by Hizbullah in their own indiscriminate attacks on Israeli civilians. In trying to slay a monster, the IDF have become monsters themselves.

Later that day, in New York, the UN Security Council adopts Resolution 1052 of 1996 which calls for a ceasefire between Lebanon and Israel. The 'Israeli Lebanon Ceasefire Understanding' will come into being at 4.30 AM on 26 April. In Egypt, a young man called Mohammed Atta is watching the television images from Qana. He pledges himself to Jihad at that moment. Swearing revenge for the dead at Qana and vowing to attack the United States. Five years later Atta will fly a hijacked airliner into the Twin Towers in New York. In doing so he will murder thousands more innocent victims. Many of whom are fellow Muslims. Many of whom are Irish.

Shortly after the massacre at Qana – in August of 1996 – a relatively unknown extremist, Osama bin Laden, cites Qana in his Fatwa and declaration of war by Al Qaeda on the United States and Israel. Addressing Al Qaeda, he states, 'Your blood has been spilt in Palestine and Iraq and the horrific image of the massacre in Qana in Lebanon are still fresh in our minds.' The cycle of violence which has gathered pace in the wadis and villages of Lebanon will culminate in the World Trade Centre attacks of 9/11 in 2001. This in turn will spawn the Global War on Terror – the longest war in American history. I could not have known then how these events would impact on my own life and how they would determine my own personal and professional development over the coming decade.

Khalid played Elvis Presley's *Greatest Hits* over and over throughout that day. Amid the chaos, Elvis sang:

> *When I first saw you, with your smile so tender,*
> *My heart was captured, My soul surrendered.*

The only other record we had was Frank Sinatra's *Greatest Hits*. That night I listened to him sing Cole Porter's 'Night and Day', again and again. It seemed to echo the blurring of night into day, the endless violence. The endless patrolling.

A week later, I was at home. Walking up Grafton Street. I deployed out of Al Yatun on the first troop rotation within days of Qana.

# Chapter 30

# Home

*Do not speak unless spoken to*

After the attack at Qana, the attacks in Irishbatt's AO dwindle to almost nothing. A strange quiet descends. I am informed by the Battalion Executive Officer that I'm rotating home on the first Chalk.

I go to my billet and pack my things. Soiled uniforms and diaries stuffed into my kitbag. I go out to the rear of the post and burn all of the letters from home. I burn everything. I burn the letters and Christmas cards and little notes that my mother has sent me. I watch it all burn. I burn the prayer to St Anthony she sent me. I burn the little prayer book of St Thérèse of Lisieux that she sent me. And I cry through the smoke and wipe the tears away on the back of my sleeve.

I then go back to my deserted billet. There is no water in Al Yatun and I haven't had a shower in ten days or so. I have one last bottle of water. I take off my tired combats in the gloom. I then open my precious bottle of water and wash myself. Carefully cupping the water in my hands, I wash the dirt and dust and smoke of Lebanon off me. I pour the last of the water over me. I'm thirsty. But I'm cleansed.

In the last hour in Al Yatun, I have a drink with Commandant McManus. There might be no water, but there's plenty of whiskey. 'Don't forget to invite me to the wedding,' he says to me as I walk out of the Communications Centre towards the vehicle park for the last time. I shake hands with BS Begley. I shake hands with Sergeant Bracken. Corporal Kennedy and Corporal Smith are on patrol.

We leave Irishbatt and the rotation convoy heads east towards the Israeli border through Bayt Yahoun and on to Saff al Hawa. We pass under the compounds. They are deserted. Silent. I watch them recede in the rear view mirror. Best view of them I've ever had. We then loop west back towards the Mediterranean and move north up the coast road to Beirut.

Beirut International Airport is deserted when we arrive. Some of the hangars and warehouses at the perimeter are still smouldering from Israeli air strikes. We dismount from the same Renault four-wheel-drive trucks that had delivered us to Irishbatt seven months previously.

We wait by the side of the tarmac on a swathe of scorched yellow and brown grass. An Israeli gunboat is clearly visible just off the coast. A black silhouette on the glittering surface of the Mediterranean. A rumour makes its way through the assembled troops. The latest word – according to the more nervous among us – is that Aer Lingus will be unable to land in Beirut. 'Too bleedin' dangerous.'

As we gaze through the hazy sunshine at the Israeli gunboat, there is a sudden exclamation. 'Here comes the plane.' We squint out to the west. Sure enough, there is a speck in the sky. Growing larger. Slowly, agonizingly slowly, the speck grows to a dot. The dot consolidates and metamorphoses into the outline of a passenger jet. Descending towards Beirut, we can now make out the familiar green and white livery of Aer Lingus. We start cheering.

The Airbus taxis to a halt. Through the shimmering heat we see our replacements filing uncertainly out of the aircraft. In the distance I hear the CS in charge of the convoy shouting, 'GET A FUCKIN' MOVE ON.' We watch as they move across the tarmac to the waiting lines of military police and logistics personnel. In turn, we see them shuffle in line towards the convoy of white painted Renault trucks. There is no cat calling from us however. Just silence.

We are called to board the aircraft. As we mount the steps we are quizzed by a new set of Military Police. 'Are you carryin guns, rifles, pistols or firearms of any kind including pen guns? Are you carrying plants, animals, birds or living creatures? Are you carrying poultry?' Surprisingly, no one is carrying a live chicken or lethal fountain pen. We step forward.

I meet Fergus just inside the aircraft. We sit next to each other in the fifth row. I have the window seat. The Aer Lingus hostesses smile at us. In their green uniforms. There is Irish music piped through the PA system. I'm pinching myself. I keep looking out the window at the smoke rising up from the ruined out-buildings and back at the Aer Lingus crew. It is surreal. The Captain comes over the PA. *Fáilte ar bord gach duine.* In just a few moments we will be cleared for take off. If you could pay attention to the safety brief, we should be underway shortly. The weather in Dublin . . . '

We cannot hear anything else as the troops have broken into a spontaneous cheer. A roar. A collective release of tension. We taxi across the choppy concrete surface and the aircraft accelerates towards the sea. As we lift off the ground, I get a last look at Lebanon. Beirut is obscured by a heat haze. The only features are plumes of smoke from fires burning slowly below. Fergus is nearly on top of me, looking over my shoulder at the scene below. 'Peacekeeping,' he says. 'Funny business.'

Some hours later we touch down in Dublin airport. The door to the aircraft is opened. A senior officer from Defence Forces headquarters enters the aircraft. He is given the microphone by the lead steward. Over the public address he tells us to 'Sit down and listen up.' There is silence. He speaks slowly and deliberately into the microphone. 'OK. Listen up. The Taoiseach John Bruton will shake hands with each of you as you disembark. Do not engage the Taoiseach in conversation. Do not speak unless spoken to. Do not talk to anyone in the airport about your deployment. Under no circumstances is anyone to talk to the media about any aspect of your trip. Do not pose for photographs unless I tell you to.' Fergus raises an eyebrow and glances over at me. Some things never change it seems.

We file out of the aircraft. We each shake hands with the Taoiseach. He has a word for each of us. Full eye contact.

It feels indescribably good to be at home again. I'm sure I'm not the only one who is tempted to kiss the ground. We are processed through the airport. Then bussed to McKee Barracks on Blackhorse Avenue. I take my kit bag. I sling it over my shoulder and walk out the gate. And there she is. Somehow, miraculously, my girlfriend is waiting for me. In her little red Ford Fiesta. 'You didn't think I'd make you get a taxi, did you?' she says. And we drive off, literally, into the sunset.

# Chapter 31

# A Farewell to Arms

*Be at the bursting doors of doom, and in the dark deliver us,*
*Who loosen the last window on the sun of sudden death.*

Prayer to St Barbara, International Patron Saint of Artillery
and those at risk of sudden death

After Lebanon, I returned to duty as an instructor in the School of
Artillery. A part of the newly evolving Combat Support College of the
Defence Forces. Or the School of Bangs as we used to call it. Sergeant
Bracken was posted to duty there also. I was very happy to be working
with him again. In the Autumn of 1996, I started a PhD in Dublin City
University. Having finished the MA in Communications prior to my
tour of duty in Lebanon, I saw the doctorate as a natural progression. I
thought it would be good for my promotion prospects. Hey, one day I
might even be Chief of Staff. I chose to research the status of women in
the Irish Armed Forces. At the time there were only 123 female personnel
in the Irish armed forces. I thought that this sample size would make
them ideal for an in-depth ethnographic study. A complete change from
the School of Bangs.

Dublin City University accepted my research proposal. Some weeks
later, following a lengthy and time consuming process – via the 'chain of
command' – I eventually got written permission from the Director of

Training to start the study. And so, I started my researches in earnest. When not doing security duties or other work, I painstakingly gathered together all of the documents related to the service of female personnel in the Irish military. This included every regulation, standard operating procedure and memorandum in relation to the recruitment, training, deployment and promotion of women in the Irish armed forces. The audit of documents also encompassed those held in Military Archives in Cathal Brugha Barracks in Dublin. I enjoyed sifting through the documents in the calm silence of the Military Archives. An oasis of sorts.

I also carried out an exhaustive comparative analysis of the conditions of service for women soldiers in the British armed forces and the US military. In addition, I conducted an in-depth examination of the conditions of service for women in An Garda Síochána – Ireland's police force – and the Royal Ulster Constabulary, the police force of Northern Ireland. I was a busy boy. And, I was proud of my progress. At each of my annual performance appraisal interviews, I made sure to include my doctoral research under the heading of 'Other Achievements During the Reporting Period.' So far, so good. My commanding officers seemed happy with my studies as long as they didn't interfere with my security duties or regimental commitments.

Those commitments were significant. In addition to security duties, I was also busy running military courses and exercises in the Artillery School. The courses revolved around the Irish Army's 105mm Royal Ordnance field gun and its 120mm Heavy Mortars. Ironically, I enjoyed the heavy artillery shoots in the Wicklow Mountains. It was strangely cathartic. Therapeutic. I was happy to see the ordnance go up-range for a change. Much better than being on the receiving end in the impact area. Those days and nights in the Glen of Imaal were a strange respite from the experience in Lebanon. Firing, instead of being fired at. But, somewhere, somehow, deep in my subconscious, I knew it was a post-ponement of sorts. Unbeknownst to me at the time, deep seeds of doubt had been sown within me in Lebanon. I was just vaguely aware of a faint uneasiness growing within me about all that had happened.

By 1998, my Mum's condition was reasonably stable. And I was getting married. To the girl in the red Ford Fiesta. It was the happiest, most exciting time of my life. It was good to be alive.

And yet there was something bothering me. Before Lebanon, I used to dream sometimes about sitting the Leaving Cert. I'd be there at the exam centre in my pyjamas or something. A classic stress dream that would recur maybe once or twice a year. And when I'd get up, I'd laugh at the silliness of it. The relief flooding through with wakefulness. At around about this time however, those quaint dreams were slowly replaced by dreams of Lebanon. I'd dream that I was in Al Yatun. I'd be wondering where my combats were. Wondering why I was heading out on patrol in my jeans. And why was Al Yatun full of kids? And why were they staring at me? Especially the little guy in the T-Shirt with the cold sores on his lips. And then I'd wake up and be relieved that I wasn't stuck in Al Yatun for seven months. I didn't find the dreams funny though. They didn't make me laugh. I'd be off form . Just a little bit. Almost imperceptibly. I didn't think much about those dreams at the time. They sneaked up on me. Slowly but surely.

In the summer of 1998, I was promoted to the rank of Captain. The Adjutant of my unit congratulated me. 'Well done Clonan. You've gone from top of the Lieutenant shit-heap to bottom of the Captain shit-heap.' I walked out of the Executive Officer's office with my shiny new rank markings. I met my old friend and mentor Sergeant Bracken as I walked across the square. Uncharacteristically for him, he gave me a stiff parade ground salute from about twenty paces away. As he got closer however, he looked at me mischievously. 'Ah, it's only you. I thought it was someone important.'

I was transferred out of the School of Bangs not long afterwards. Transferred from Kildare to the Second Field Artillery Regiment in McKee Barracks, Dublin. I spent six months in the 2nd Regiment as a Battery Commander. I was briefly reunited there with Corporal Kennedy. It was the first time we'd met since Qana. He greeted me with a wide beatific smile and showed me his knuckles. 'What do you think of them knuckles now?' I stared carefully and then the penny dropped. Where once was tattooed 'LOVE' and 'HATE' across the knuckles, there was now just a series of faint, pink scars. 'I got the tattoos lasered off with me overseas allowances,' he said. 'And another thing. I've only gone and done me Leavin' Cert.' A few months after I arrived in the unit, Corporal Kennedy left the Defence Forces. He got his leaving certificate results as a mature student in August of 1998. That October, he started full-time as a student in University College, Dublin. In time, he completed his degree to work as a social worker with troubled youth in north County Dublin. He told me that he had bumped into Sergeant Fuckin-Fuck's daughter in the Arts Block in Trinity. 'She doesn't curse at all.'

In late 1998, I was called to a meeting in the Registrar's office in DCU. As part of the ongoing review of my academic progress, I was advised that it would be prudent to get a further letter of consent from the Chief of Staff in order that my doctoral research into female soldiers be examined and then lodged to the library in DCU. I sought an interview with the Chief of Staff and I was given written permission to have the work examined and lodged to the university's library.

In December 1998, shortly after this fortuitous meeting with the Chief of Staff, I was transferred into the Defence Forces Press Office in the Chief of Staff's Branch. This was my dream job. So far, so great. Here

I was, just two years after Lebanon, getting married, doing a doctorate, promoted to rank of Captain and working directly for the Chief of Staff. What could possibly go wrong?

Between 1998 and 2000, I travelled back to Lebanon and Syria many times. Usually accompanying journalists who were covering our operations there. In 1999, I witnessed the final withdrawal of Israeli troops from Lebanon. And I saw the compounds finally dismantled. The Cuckoo's Nest was flattened. Gone forever. I've since been told that Hizbullah have erected a ferris wheel on top of the hill where Brashit Compound or DFF 23 once stood. If I ever want to give myself PTSD I think, I'll go for a ride on that rickety Ferris Wheel.

During one of those trips to Lebanon, in the Summer of 1999, the Directorate of Operations gave me permission to interview female personnel serving in the Lebanon about their experiences of overseas service. As part of my ongoing research journey into women soldiers, I had begun interviewing female soldiers of all ranks in various units at home in Ireland about their experiences of military life in the Irish armed forces. The interviews were deeply disturbing. The women I spoke to were passionate about their military careers, but were equally passionate and enraged about their experiences of discrimination. And worse. Many spoke to me of bullying, sexual harassment, sexual assault. There were even allegations of rape.

All of this came as a complete and total shock to me. I had never been bullied in the Army. Quite the opposite. I had been recognized, validated, promoted and educated by the Irish Army. I had been mentored and encouraged by my fellow officers. I had depended on them in Lebanon. I trusted them completely. We literally put our lives on the line for each other. The Army was an extension of my family. So, for me, the concept of bullying within the Army simply did not exist. I had never been harassed or sexually assaulted. So, therefore, in my mind the concept of sexual harassment and sexual assault within the military just did not, could not, exist.

And yet, almost all of the women that I spoke to spoke to me about experiences of sexual discrimination, sexual harassment and sexual assault. I spoke to my supervisor in DCU about the unexpected direction that the research was taking. We considered the ethical implications of the work. All of the women who spoke of sexual assault had reported matters to the military police. Sadly, none of them expressed confidence in the Army's reporting and grievance procedures. We felt that it was essential therefore that we prepare the fullest and most comprehensive account of the problem as possible. This would be the only way to present the issue in its fullest historical and contemporary context in order to formulate and recommend solutions to the military authorities.

In the meantime, in the autumn and winter of 1999 and throughout 2000, I informed my immediate superiors of the serious and pressing concerns raised by our female comrades. Our sisters in arms. My immediate superiors at the time were very supportive and had encouraged my research activities at all times. They urged me to complete the investigation thoroughly and to prepare a comprehensive report for the Chief of Staff. This I did.

At around this time, however, I began to realise that perhaps I was no longer suited to military service. Doing the doctoral research had brought with it the realisation that I could no longer serve as an army officer in the Irish Defence Forces. I craved autonomy. I needed the kind of self-realisation and freedom of action that was not possible within the restrictions imposed by military law. I had simply moved on.

In addition, we were expecting our first child – due in December of 2000. And therefore on a pragmatic and practical level, I also needed to work in a more family-friendly environment. For whilst the Army is many things – family-friendly it is not. And so, for a constellation of reasons, I found myself in November of 2000 filling out an application form to retire from the organisation that had been of such central importance in my life for over a decade.

Officer's Records accepted my application to retire. Their only observation to me was that I had failed to apply in writing to get married. Permission was granted to me retrospectively. My PhD was lodged to the library of DCU in December of 2000. I retired, took a big drop in salary and began lecturing in communications theory in the Institute of Technology sector.

Ten months later, in October of 2001 the Minister for Defence ordered an official inquiry into my research. The Study Review Group reported two years later. Their report vindicated my findings and the Defence Forces have since put in place almost all of my original recommendations in relation to equality and dignity in the workplace. As a result, the Defence Forces is a better place to work for the thousands of men and women in the regular army and reserves who serve in Irish uniform. In fact the Irish military, as a direct consequence, are considered world leaders in terms of their dignity at work and equality policies. So, all's well that ends well.

# Chapter 32

# Births and Deaths

*Forget about it*

Darach is born on 10 December, 2000. Our Millennium baby. Our first born. For me, as a newly expectant father, the pregnancy is a strangely abstract experience. Looking at a tiny new person on a scan in the Coombe Hospital. Seeing the heart beat in a blurred grey-black aqueous medium. Listening to the insistent rhythmic sound of life on the foetal heart monitor.

At night, though, feeling his soft kicks in the darkness with my hand on his mother's tummy, he becomes real. Tiny ripples of movement. I can feel him now.

And, finally the delivery. The sudden surge and twisting motion as he unwinds and slips from the womb. Crying in the unaccustomed glare of the lights in the delivery suite. Our hearts racing. A boy. A baby boy.

Something within me changes. Something shifts. Later that night, as I am driving towards home, I catch a glimpse of that necklace of lights around Dublin Bay. That sacred semi-circle of orange streetlight stretching from Howth Head around to Dalkey and Bray. I take in the red lights winking at me from Pigeon House. I look out beyond the hazy orange upwash of Dublin's light pollution into the sudden and seemingly infinite inky black of the Irish sea. And I know then that I have fallen in love. In a way that has taken me completely by surprise. And in that moment, I know that I will go to the ends of the earth for my baby boy. And even though he is just hours, just minutes old, I know I will love him unconditionally until the end of time.

And in that coming of age, I remember another newborn baby. That tiny baby thrust into my arms in Al Yatun just four years previously. As a young soldier, I could not have known what fear that woman felt. As a father, on this night, four years later, she becomes fully human. For the first time.

As a younger man, in that Easter of 1996, I had had an introduction to anarchy. To chaos. I felt myself familiar with death. Or so I thought.

And in particular, in that one house, in Jumay Jumay, the dead family lying – in various poses – around the evening meal. The corpses immaculate. Untouched. Corporal Kennedy whistling throughout, 'They didn't even get to eat their fucking dinner.'

So, that was my introduction to death. A baptism of fire if you like. And in the Holy Land. How appropriate for a boy educated by the Christian Brothers. To be introduced to the sacred mysteries among the lemon groves and olive trees around Tyre and Sidon.

When I eventually got home that Easter, my father had advised me not to talk about it. 'Forget about it,' was his shouted advice. He was a hard man. He knew what he was talking about, I thought. So, I did. I buried it deep. 'Don't mention the war', so to speak. But, it resurrects itself. It sneaks up on me and taps me on the shoulder from time to time.

My mum's cancer reasserts itself in 2002. In March of 2003, Corporal Kennedy calls me out of the blue. Uncharacteristically distraught, he tells me, 'Me Ma's dead, Tom. She just dropped dead in Top of the Pops on Gardiner Street. She was buying Kerr's Pinks when it happened.' My own beloved mother – despite her promise to me as a small boy – also dies unexpectedly at the same time.

She had been sent by ambulance to the Mater Hospital suffering from 'joint pain.' When I get there Bláithín is no longer herself. Stroked out. Her mouth, a curious 'O' shape. A shape that I recognise to be 'a precursor to death' – as Sergeant Bracken has told me in a different life. Blunt but accurate. My sister is there when she slips away. Holding her hand when she sighs and ceases to be. This is of some comfort. To think that one of us was there.

That night, my father asks us all to leave the small hospital room where my mum had spent her last few hours. He wants to say goodbye 'in private.' I watch him through the glass in the door. And I see him simply say, 'Goodbye Bláithín.' He catches me looking of course. As he brushes past me, he briefly holds eye contact. And he tells me – fiercely, intensely – 'Your mother died just as she lived. Politely.' He is right. But she never said goodbye. And when the time came, neither did he.

In the nights leading up to Bláithín's death – the aforementioned 'precursor' – I lie awake in bed. Thinking and worrying. Because this was death in slow motion – not like in the Lebanon. I roll over very gently in the witching hours and put my hand on my wife's swollen tummy. And I feel the little feathery movements of my daughter in there. Tiny kicks. Ripples across the skin surface. Little Liadain inside her. In her waterworld. New life.

Meanwhile, Bláithín is laid out in the family home. She died on the Thursday night – but can't be buried until the Tuesday because of the St Patrick's Day weekend. My Dad is worried. 'Should I turn off the heat?' he'd asked the man from the funeral home. 'Don't worry about that Eugene,' the undertaker intones, 'she's well looked after in that regard.' Later, over a cigarette, my father speculates at length about what exactly that meant. If nothing else, he was always intellectually curious.

When the coffin is finally lowered, I feel relieved.

And then – just a week later – I get a call to go to the Coombe. Liadain is dead too. She'd stopped kicking and swimming. Perfectly still. They induce her that evening. And unlike the other four births, it is a completely silent labour. No cries. No sound at all. Just me and Liadain's Mum and the medics. I hear the whispered phrase, 'Cord accident.'

Naively, I had brought a red and white candy stripe cotton vest for Liadain. It had been our favourite on the boys. It won't fit Liadain. I can see that immediately in the delivery room. She is perfectly formed but so very small. The nurses make a little dress for her from some floral curtain material and we fasten it around her with a safety pin. The nurses give us a Polaroid camera and advise us to take some photographs. 'You'll be glad later.'

So, in the dark, in the delivery room, we take flash photographs of our little Liadain. Already gone. Already the grey lady. The nurses give us a small cardboard box with some towels. 'When you are finished saying goodbye, you can bring her to the nurses' station and we'll look after her.'

Finally, we place our little girl – very carefully – into the box. I arrange the towels and walk through the busy labour ward to the nurses' station. Past women and girls clutching their tummies. Past the anxious Dads pacing the hall. Holding the box that held our hopes and dreams.

Two days later we drive little Liadain to the Little Angels Plot in Glasnevin cemetery. The tiny white coffin balanced on her mum's knees in the car. We drive in silence. Stop at the red lights. Go on green. On through Phibsboro and on to Glasnevin. A young man with a shovel over his shoulder meets us and walks ahead of us to the spot. He speaks gently to us and indicates where the hole in the ground is. 'Say goodbye in your own time,' he says. 'Take all the time you need.'

The crows caw in the trees. The wind chimes chime in the branches. Liadain's Mum weeps. Liadain's milk seeping through her black dress. And we place the little coffin – so very gently – into the wet soil.

And placing Liadain there the world keeps going round. It doesn't stop for even a moment. Revolving around the sun and spinning and drifting onwards towards whatever distant stars. But I am rooted to the spot. I can't stand up. It is impossible to stand up and turn away. And walk away. Leaving our precious little daughter in the ground like that. And I think of all the other little bundles I had seen as a young man in Lebanon. And I think of the Lebanese men and women I had seen at the edge of bombed out ruins – their shoulders stooped in grief and disbelief. And I think of how I have finally joined them as brothers and sisters in all of our weeping and sorrow and loss. And when I can't sleep for grieving, echoing back to me from all of those nights in Al Yatun, I hear the words of Cole Porter's 'Night and Day'.

*Night and day, you are the one*
*only you beneath the moon or under the sun*
*whether near to me or far*
*it's no matter darling*
*where you are*
*I think of you*
*day and night, night and day*

# Chapter 33

# Post Script

And even my Dad died, despite being a chain-smoking tough guy. All that was left of him was his dentures. And his pyjamas. After all those years – decades – of smoking and shouting and living on the edge. I was sent up from accident and emergency to his hospital room –where he had been admitted for tests – to collect his 'final effects.' They hadn't been able to wake him after his tea. Mind you, he was just skin and bone at that stage. He was almost dead anyhow.

His last words to me were about the jelly he'd been getting in hospital. 'I haven't had jelly since your mother died . . . Of course, you'd never make me jelly . . . Too fucking busy.' And irony of ironies, after his last supper – there was the jelly on his hospital tray. Uneaten.


Rshaf, Bayt Yahun, Shaqrah, Jumay Jumay, Majdal Silm. Those names as familiar to me now as Glasnevin, Phibsboro, Constitution Hill, the North Quays. Lebanese villages I patrolled night after night after night during the winter and spring of 1996. I still recite the names – like the sorrowful mysteries – sleeping, moonlit villages with whom I became so intimately acquainted.

Fifteen years later, my dreams of Lebanon are recurring. Fifteen years later, when I wake at four in the morning, I listen. As the house sighs and as my four children sleep, I think of Rshaf, Bayt Yahun, Shaqrah, Jumay Jumay and Majdal Silm. In my mind's eye I work the battalion patrol plan and report my position on the Motorola. I think of the young man that I was then. I think of my parents, long dead. I think of my little girl. And I think of all those passed over and gone. And I wonder what part of my heart was left in Lebanon, what part of my soul surrendered there.

And on those rare occasions when I meet Sergeant Bracken, he reminds me, 'Those were the good old days, weren't they?' And we both laugh. All the way to Tibnine. All the way to Glasnevin cemetery. All the way from Dublin to Beirut and back. Forty thousand Irish troops served in Lebanon. Forty-seven died there. Not everyone comes home. And nobody comes home the same.